INVESTMENTS
PROBLEM SOLVER

INVESTMENTS PROBLEM SOLVER

Dilip D. Kare
SunBank Fellow of Finance
University of North Florida

Prentice Hall
Englewood Cliffs, NJ 07632

Library of Congress Cataloging-in-Publication Data

Kare, Dilip D.
    Investments problem solver [computer file] / Dilip D. Kare.
    1 computer disk : 3.5 in. + 1 manual.
    System requirements: IBM or compatible; 384K RAM; 360K floppy disk
drive; MS-DOS or PC-DOS 2.1 or higher.
    Title from title screen.
    Summary: Stand-alone flexible software for investment problem
solving.
    ISBN 0-13-481920-9
    1. Investment analysis—Software. I. Title.
HG4529 ‹MRCRR›
332.6—dc12   92–27437
                                  CIP

Limit of Liability and Disclaimer of Warranty:

The Author and Publisher have used their best efforts in preparing this book and the examples/exercises contained in it. These efforts include the development, research, and testing of the theories to determine their effectiveness.

The Author and Publisher make no warranty of any kind, expressed or implied, with respect to the documentation in this book. The Author and Publisher shall not be liable in any event for incidental or consequential damages in connection with, or arising from the furnishing, performance, or use of these examples/exercises.

Acquisition Editor: Leah Jewell
Production Editors: Fred Dahl and Rose Kernan
Copy Editor: Rose Kernan
Designers: Fred Dahl and Rose Kernan
Cover Designer: Lundgren Graphics Ltd.
Prepress Buyer: Trudy Pisciotti
Manufacturing Buyer: Robert Anderson
Supplements Editor: Jennifer Fisher

 © 1993 by Prentice-Hall, Inc.
A Division of Simon & Schuster
Englewood Cliffs, New Jersey 07632

Printed in the United States of America
10 9 8 7 6 5 4 3 2 1

ISBN 0-13-481920-9

Prentice-Hall International (UK) Limited, London
Prentice-Hall of Australia Pty. Limited, Sydney
Prentice-Hall Canada Inc., Toronto
Prentice-Hall Hispanoamericana, S.A., Mexico
Prentice-Hall of India Private Limited, New Delhi
Prentice-Hall of Japan, Inc., Tokyo
Simon & Schuster Asia Pte. Ltd., Singapore
Editora Prentice-Hall do Brasil, Ltda., Rio de Janeiro

To my mother, Laxmi

Contents

Preface

Modern investment theory is very quantitative in nature. Problems based on portfolio theory, capital markets theory, or options theory can sometimes require complex and tedious computations. In my experience as an instructor, I found that students confronted with such computations in practice problems are sometimes reluctant to spend time crunching numbers.

Fortunately, the development and the widespread availability of personal computers provide both students and instructors with a great deal of help in number crunching. Today, most investment texts are accompanied by software that is designed to help in problem solving. However, most of this software is in the form of spreadsheet templates applicable to specific problems in one text book. The software requires the user to have access to a commercial spreadsheet package which can be expensive and require a large investment in sophisticated hardware.

These drawbacks of using spreadsheet templates for problem solving inspired me to develop **Investments Problem Solver**. The main purpose of developing this software was to make available to students and instructors a software that is stand-alone (i.e., that can run directly from DOS), flexible, and easy to use. The interface and data entry screens were designed so as to make the software very user-friendly. The use of menus makes it easy to navigate around the numerous applications in the software. The design of the software is such that it can run even on the first generation personal computer. All the hardware that a user needs is 256K of RAM and a floppy-disk drive.

It is my hope that students will use **Investments Problem Solver** as a learning tool to eliminate the tedium of repetitive number crunching. Both students and instructors can use the software not only to speed up the problem solution process, but also to develop an understanding of the underlying concepts by using sensitivity analysis techniques.

Acknowledgments

I would like to thank several individuals for their support and assistance in this project. Leah Jewell and Diane DeCastro, both of Prentice Hall facilitated the reviews of the software and its publication. Also, I want to thank Whitney Blake (formerly with Prentice Hall) for her help in getting this project off the ground.

My friend and colleague, Richard White, provided me with the encouragement to begin writing this software. Debbie Karst was a big help in getting the manuscript ready. Edward Moses and Tony Herbst tested the software and made valuable suggestions. Thanks are due to my wife, Grace, for copyediting this manuscript. Finally, I want to thank the reviewers for their constructive criticism and suggestions. They are as follows: Gilbert W. Bickum of Eastern Kentucky University, Henry R. Oppenheimer of University of Rhode Island, Adam K. Gehr, Jr. of DePaul University, Tony R. Wingler of University of North Carolina, James F. Feller of Middle Tennessee State University, James Shaw of University of San Francisco, and James K. Seward of Dartmouth College.

Dilip D. Kare

1 *About the Software*

Because of the widespread availability of personal computers, the teaching methods used in computation-intensive courses such as investments and portfolio analysis have undergone a major change. Instructors and students now can leave the computations to computers and concentrate on discussing the theoretical aspects of investments. **Investment Problem Solver** is intended to help the student as well as the instructor in solving a wide variety of problems encountered in a typical course in investments and portfolio analysis.

Investment Problem Solver differs from the software packages normally available with investment text books in one important respect. Most, if not all, software packages accompanying investment textbooks are simply collections of Lotus 1-2-3™ templates designed to solve specific problems in a particular textbook. Because of this, the use of the software package is limited to solving problems from that particular textbook. Another problem with such software is that the user must have access to Lotus 1-2-3™, which is an expensive software program which can run only on personal computers equipped with a large RAM and a hard drive.

Investment Problem Solver is designed to eliminate these problems. It is a freestanding software program which *does not need any other software (except DOS) to execute*. The program is custom designed using Turbo Pascal™ (a programming language from Borland International) for students taking courses in investments and in security analysis and portfolio management. Therefore, it is easy to use, it's flexible, and it is very user-friendly. Data entry screens are designed to prompt the user to enter data in the correct format. The user is prevented from accidentally entering data in a wrong format. Finally, wherever possible, every effort has been made to provide all the intermediate calculation steps in the solution procedure.

Another advantage of **Investment Problem Solver** is that it can be executed from personal computers equipped with the minimum RAM (384K) and only one floppy-disk drive. This makes the software package available even to students who do not have access to sophisticated, state-of-the-art personal computers.

ORGANIZATION

Investment Problem Solver is structured as an integrated package which consists of five application modules. This makes switching from one application to another a simple matter involving two or three keystrokes. Figure 1.1 explains the organization of the program in a tree diagram.

The five modules in the program are:

1. Financial Mathematics
2. Bond Analysis
3. Common Stock Analysis
4. Hybrid Securities
5. Portfolio Theory

Module number 1, Financial Mathematics, deals with the fundamental concept of the time value of money. The user may calculate present values and future values of different types of cash flows. The Bond Analysis module allows the user to solve problems in bond pricing, yield-to-maturity, and duration. The Common Stock Analysis module can be used to tackle problems in margin analysis, holding period yield, zero/constant growth stock pricing, and non-constant growth stock pricing. The Hybrid Securities module handles call option pricing, the put-call parity theorem, implied volatility of the underlying security, and convertible bond problems. The Portfolio Theory module can be applied to problems in risk-return analysis, expected returns and standard deviation of returns, beta estimation, estimation of standard deviation of returns for portfolios of up to five securities, estimation of the minimum risk portfolios and portfolio performance evaluation.

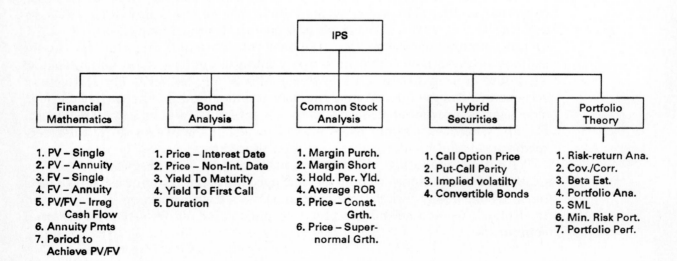

HARDWARE AND SOFTWARE REQUIREMENTS

In order to make the **Investment Problem Solver** accessible to all students, it is designed to run on any IBM compatible computer. It runs equally well on a computer equipped with the Intel 8086 or 8088 microprocessor as it does on a computer equipped with the faster microprocessors like the 80286, 80386SX, or 80386. The speed of execution of the program will depend upon the type of microprocessor installed in the computer.

The program can be executed on a computer fitted with only one floppy-disk drive. If the computer is fitted with a hard-disk drive then the user is better off running the program from the hard disk. The program requires only 384 Kilo bytes of main memory (RAM) to run.

Also, there are also no restrictions as to the type of monitor required since the program runs on monochrome monitors (amber or green) with or without a graphics adaptor board, as well as on color monitors equipped with either CGA, EGA, or VGA standard graphic adaptor boards.

Since the software was designed for use as a freestanding program, the only other software needed to operate the **Investment Problem Solver** is DOS, Version 2.1 or later (PC-DOS or MS-DOS).

EXECUTION FROM A FLOPPY-DISK DRIVE

The execution of the program from a floppy-disk drive is quite simple. Insert the program disk in the floppy-disk drive (assumed to be drive A) and close the latch. Enter the following commands in the computer in sequence to execute the program. (The following discussion assumes that the computer is equipped with a hard-disk drive and that the default drive after boot up is C.)

```
C>A: ⟨Enter⟩   (This command is not needed if the boot drive is Drive A)
A>IPS ⟨Enter⟩
```

After the second command is entered, the computer will read the program file from the program disk. This operation may take a few seconds. Once the entire program is read into the RAM, the introductory screen will appear with the title and copyright notice at the bottom. Users of a computer equipped with a graphic adaptor board and a color monitor will view a blue screen with the title in large letters in white. The first screen on a monochrome monitor not equipped with a graphics adaptor board will be much plainer in appearance. The first screen will remain visible for a few seconds after which the main menu will appear on the screen. The operation of the user interface, which allows access to the desired module from the software, will be discussed later in this chapter.

INSTALLATION ON A HARD-DISK DRIVE

If the student owns a computer fitted with a hard-disk drive, it is preferable to install and execute the program from the hard disk. Because the data transfer rate of a hard-disk drive is substantially greater than the data transfer rate of a floppy-disk drive, programs executed from a hard disk (or hard drive) will load and execute much faster than those executed from a floppy disk.

The installation of the program on a hard drive involves creating a subdirectory on the hard disk, copying all the files from the program disk into the subdirectory, and creating a batch file that will help the user execute the program with one command from the root directory. The following sequence of commands will accomplish all these tasks. Once again, it is assumed that the floppy-disk drive in which the program disk will be placed for copying the files is designated as the A drive and the hard-disk drive is the C drive.

```
C:>md ip  ⟨Enter⟩  [create a subdirectory called ip]
C:>copy a:*.*  \ip\*.* ⟨Enter⟩  [copy files in the subdirectory]
```

At this point, the subdirectory is created and the files are copied into it. Next, the batch file to run the program from the root directory will be created with the following commands:

```
C:> copy con ip.bat ⟨Enter⟩
    echo off⟨Enter⟩
    cd ip    ⟨Enter⟩
    ips      ⟨Enter⟩
    cd\      ⟨Enter⟩
    ^Z       ⟨Enter⟩
```

The final command, "^Z" (the end-of-file marker), is typed by pressing the control key (marked with "Ctrl") and the "Z" key simultaneously. The user is required to press the enter key after typing each command. This sequence of commands will create and save a batch file called **ip.bat**. Once this file is created, the user can execute **Investment Problem Solver** directly from the root directory by simply entering the command **ip**. At this point, the blue screen with titles in white letters will appear. After a few seconds, the main menu will appear on the screen. Once the user terminates the program, control of the computer is returned to DOS at the root directory level.

OPERATION OF THE USER INTERFACE

The user interface is that part of a computer program which allows the user to communicate with the program. It involves tasks like indicating the selection of the proper module, data entry and editing, printing results, and so on.

In modern programming practice, more attention is paid to the design of the user interface than any other part of the program. It is estimated that 80 percent of the code is devoted to the user interface and the remaining 20 percent to the main task of the program like data analysis and manipulation. Without a properly designed user interface, a program will be very difficult to use.

Investment Problem Solver uses two types of menus which offer a choice among different courses of action. The first type is a vertical menu with a highlight bar that can be moved up and down in order to highlight different selections. In this type of menu, the user is asked to select one of the various application modules available. The main menu is an example of this type of menu (see Figure 1.2).

It allows the user to select the type of problem needed to be solved—a problem on time value of money, a bond problem, a common stock problem, a problem on hybrid securities (options or convertible bonds), or a problem in portfolio analysis. The final choice is to return to DOS. When this menu appears on the screen, one may use the space bar, the up and down arrow keys, the ⟨**Escape**⟩ key, the ⟨**Home**⟩ key, the ⟨**End**⟩ key, or the ⟨**Enter**⟩ key. Pressing any other key at this point will cause the computer to emit a beep indicating that the user's input was not acceptable.

The space bar or the up and down arrow keys are used to move the highlight bar up and down, until the user's selection is highlighted. The ⟨**Home**⟩ key may be used to move the highlight bar to the first selection in the menu, and the ⟨**End**⟩ key to move the highlight bar to the last selection in the menu. The selection will be shown on the screen in reverse video. By pressing the ⟨**Enter**⟩ key, the user indicates his/her selection of the module. At this point, another vertical menu will appear on the screen asking the user to narrow down the choice to a specific type of problem. For example, if the user selected **BOND ANALYSIS** from the main menu, then the next vertical menu will offer the user a choice among submodules to deal with different types of bond problems such as bond valuation, YTC, YTM, duration, etc. (see Figure 1.3).

The user will then follow a procedure similar to the one previously described to indicate the choice of the submodule. This will bring up the data entry screen. A typical data entry screen is shown in Figure 1.4.

Fig. 1.2

```
         ┌─────────────────────────────────────┐
         │                                     │
         │   Investment Problems Menu          │
         │  ┌───────────────────────────────┐  │
         │  │ Financial Mathematics         │  │
         │  └───────────────────────────────┘  │
         │   Bond Analysis                     │
         │                                     │
         │   Common Stock Analysis             │
         │                                     │
         │   Analysis of Hybrid Sec.           │
         │                                     │
         │   Portfolio Theory                  │
         │                                     │
         │   Exit to DOS                       │
         │                                     │
         └─────────────────────────────────────┘
```

Use the Spacebar or ↑↓ to Move the Highlight Bar Up and Down
Make Your Choice with the <ENTER> key

Fig. 1.3

```
┌─────────────────────────────────────────┐
│                                         │
│            Bond Analysis                │
│   ┌─────────────────────────────────┐   │
│   │  Bond Price - Interest Date     │   │
│   └─────────────────────────────────┘   │
│      Bond Price - Non-Int. Date         │
│                                         │
│      Yield To Maturity                  │
│                                         │
│      Yield To First Call                │
│                                         │
│      Duration                           │
│                                         │
│      Main Menu                          │
│                                         │
└─────────────────────────────────────────┘
```

Use the Spacebar or ↑↓ to Move the Highlight Bar Up and Down
Make Your Choice with the <ENTER> key

If the user presses the ⟨**Escape**⟩ key while a vertical type of menu is active, the control of the program will be passed on to the previous menu. When the main menu is active, pressing the ⟨**Escape**⟩ key will terminate the execution of the program.

The other type of menu used in this software package is the horizontal menu with a slide bar. This menu always appears on the 24th line of the screen. If the computer is equipped with a color monitor, this menu appears as a red band. The slide bar is white in color. When this type of a menu appears on the screen, the acceptable input is limited to the space bar, the left and right arrow keys, the ⟨**Home**⟩ key, the ⟨**End**⟩ key, and the ⟨**Enter**⟩ key. The space bar or the arrow keys allow the user to move the slide bar to the intended selection. The ⟨**Home**⟩ key will move the highlight bar to the first selection in the menu and the ⟨**End**⟩ key will move the highlight bar to the last selection in the menu. Pressing the ⟨**Enter**⟩ key will cause the program to initiate the course of action which is highlighted in the menu bar. As before, if a user presses a key other than any one of those mentioned above, the computer will emit a beep indicating an unacceptable input.

Among the choices of action offered by a horizontal menu is **Print Results**. The user must switch on the printer connected to the computer and ensure that it is loaded with paper before making this choice. The program is designed to detect if the printer is not on at the time this choice is made. If the program detects that the printer is not on, it will cause the computer to emit a beep and print an error message at the bottom of the screen about switching on the printer. The user then decides to continue with printing after switching on the printer or to abort the printing of results by pressing ⟨**Escape**⟩.

The solution screen contains some graphics characters which form the border of the display. Executing the "Graphics" command from DOS before executing IPS will enable your printer to print these characters. Otherwise, the border of the solution display will not be printed as it appears on the screen.

Fig. 1.4

```
┌─────────────────────────────────────────────────┐
│                                                   │
│                   Bond Data                       │
│                                                   │
│                   Face Value ($):                 │
│                                                   │
│                 Coupon Rate (%):                  │
│                                                   │
│         Number of Coupon Pmts Remaining:          │
│                                                   │
│               Yield to Maturity (%):              │
│                                                   │
│         Number of Coupon Pmts per Year:           │
│                                                   │
└─────────────────────────────────────────────────┘
```

Please hit the <ENTER> key after entering data in each field

DATA INPUT

Investment Problem Solver is designed to be as general and flexible as possible in terms of its application to problems in investments, security analysis, and portfolio management. This means that a user will be presented with a wide variety of data entry screens when using the program. Every effort has been made to standardize the data entry screens in look and the type of input allowed.

When the user is expected to input a dollar amount, that data item description will be indicated by a dollar sign in parentheses after the item description. All dollar amounts are expected to be entered as real numbers. For example, $22-1/2 will be entered as "22.50." When the expected input is a real number, only the 10 digits (i.e., "0" to "9"), the decimal point, and the minus sign can to be used in data input. An attempt to use any other key will cause the computer to emit a beep indicating that the key used in the input is not acceptable.

When the user is asked to enter an interest rate, a rate of return, or a margin percentage, the input is expected to be in percentages. For example, if the yield-to-maturity in a bond valuation problem is given as .0978, the user must input "9.78" (without the percentage sign). All such inputs are indicated by a percentage sign in parentheses after the data description. This also applies to the entry of probabilities. In some cases, such as estimating common stock betas using regression analysis, the user is given a choice of entering returns either as percentages or as decimals. Only in the case of correlation coefficients is the user required to enter the data as decimals.

In cases where the expected input is in character form, both the lower case and the upper case characters are acceptable. Again, if the user enters an unacceptable character, the computer will beep to indicate that an error has occurred. The user is then given another chance to enter the correct inputs.

If for any reason the user wishes not to proceed with data entry while in the data entry mode, the data entry process can be terminated by pressing the ⟨**Escape**⟩ key. This will return the control of the program to the main menu of the module.

DATA EDITING

It is inevitable that some mistakes are made during data entry. The program is designed to give the user an opportunity to catch and correct data input errors before the solution to a problem is calculated with incorrect input. A menu bar will appear at the bottom of each data input screen after the data entry process is completed. The menu offers a choice between editing the input data or seeking a solution to the problem. If the user chooses the option to edit input data, the menu bar will disappear and the user will be given the opportunity to edit the first data field in the input screen. This will be indicated by the appearance of a highlight block in the entry position of data field number 1. The data already entered in this position will be shown in reverse video. At this point, the user can use the ⟨**Delete**⟩ key, the ⟨**Insert**⟩ key, or any other key on the keyboard to make the necessary changes to the data item in the first field. The user must press the ⟨**Enter**⟩ key after making the desired changes to indicate that the correction to the data item in field number 1 is over. This action will position the highlight block at the next field of data.

If no change is needed at any data position, the user can move to the next data position by pressing the ⟨**Enter**⟩ key or the down arrow key. The user may navigate up and down the data input screen by repeatedly pressing the up or down arrow keys, or the ⟨**Enter**⟩ key. When the ⟨**Enter**⟩ key is pressed at the last data entry position on the screen, the user exits the edit mode. However, if the user wishes to exit the edit mode after making only one small correction to a data field, it can be accomplished by pressing ⟨**End**⟩ at the next data field.

Once all the corrections to the input data are complete, the user's action (the ⟨**Enter**⟩ key at the last field or the ⟨**End**⟩ key on any field) will bring up the menu bar. Moving the slide bar to the choice '**Show Results**' and pressing the ⟨**Enter**⟩ key will bring up the result screen. Finally, the user can exit a submodule while in the data edit mode by pressing the ⟨**Escape**⟩ key.

Another feature of the edit capability of this program is that the user is allowed to edit the input data even after the solution screen appears. At the bottom of every solution screen, the user is presented with a number of choices. Typically, these choices are **Print Results**, **Edit Input**, **New Input** and going back to the main menu of the active module. To obtain a hard copy of the results, highlight the first choice and press the ⟨**Enter**⟩ key. This will output the solution screen to the printer. If the user wishes to edit input data, the selection of the appropriate choice on the menu bar will bring up the data entry screen once again, with all field positions showing the input data. The user can now move around the data entry screen to make the changes and take a look at the new solution by following the procedure described above. On the other hand, if the user wants to enter the data for a new problem, the option **New**

Input should be selected. This will bring up the data entry screen, but this time all the data positions on the screen will be empty.

The editing feature of the program makes it much more user-friendly. Any data input error, if detected by the user in time, can be corrected immediately. This feature can also be used to demonstrate the sensitivity of the solution of the problem to changes in different input variables.

However, some input errors are not obvious. The input data for a problem may not be in accordance with the assumptions used in the solution procedure. Errors of this type may not be easily detectable. This is where the error trapping feature of the program will prove useful.

ERROR TRAPPING

Every computer user knows the "GIGO" (Garbage In, Garbage Out) principle which implies that the quality of the output of a program is as good as the quality of the data input. This is particularly true of a software program such as **Investment Problem Solver**, which relies only on the data entered by the user to provide the results. Incorrect data input will lead to incorrect results, or in some extreme cases, may cause the computer to hang up.

Every possible care has been taken to prevent such an eventuality by making the program detect data input errors and provide the user with an opportunity to correct those errors. However, it is impossible to think of all possible input errors and some unique combinations of data input errors may still lead to the program hanging up.

One example of an input error occurs in calculating the price of a stock using the constant growth model. This model can be applied only if the growth rate in dividends is less than the required rate of return from the common stock. If the user enters a growth rate that is greater than the required rate of return, the computer will emit a beep and a message box in red will appear on the screen informing the user about the error. You are then given the opportunity to make the necessary change in the respective data items.

Another instance of the error trapping feature can be demonstrated by entering percentages for a probability distribution (in portfolio theory problems) which do not add up to 100 percent. Although this is not a fatal error, the results calculated using these data will not be accurate. The program tests for the sum of the probabilities and flashes a message on the screen if the sum is not exactly 100 percent.

2 *Financial Mathematics*

The concept of time value of money is the foundation block of the theory of finance. The valuation of common stocks, bonds, preferred stocks, and options are all based on this concept. However, most textbooks on investments, security analysis, and portfolio management pay very little attention to this topic. Nevertheless, students of investment must be familiar with this concept in order to understand the valuation of different types of securities. It is for this reason that a separate module on the topic of the time value of money is included in **Investment Problem Solver.**

This module contains the following submodules covering various applications of time value of money:

1. Present Value of a Single Cash Flow
2. Future Value of a Single Cash Flow
3. Present Value of an Ordinary Annuity/Annuity Due
4. Future Value of an Ordinary Annuity/Annuity Due
5. Present/Future Value of an Irregular Stream of Cash Flow
6. Annuity Payment Required to Obtain the Desired Present/Future Value.
7. Period Required to Achieve Present/Future Value

Submodules 1 and 2 solve problems dealing with the calculation of the present value and the future value, respectively, of a single cash flow. The submodule is designed so that the time values can be calculated at any compounding or discounting frequency desired. For the purpose of comparison, present and future value calculated with continuous discounting or compounding are also provided.

Submodules 3 and 4 handle problems on the present value/future value of annuities. Once again, different compounding/discounting frequencies can be entered. Solutions for both an ordinary annuity and an annuity due are presented.

Submodule 5 can be used to solve problems involving irregular streams of cash flows. For a student, these problems can be extremely time consuming because of the necessity of calculating the present value/future value of each cash flow. This module can handle up to 30 cash flows.

Submodule 6 can be used to calculate the annuity payment from the present/future value desired at a given interest rate. This submodule is not only of academic interest, but should also prove useful in making decisions about car loans, a mortgage on a house, and so on.

Finally, submodule 7 can be used to estimate the time required to achieve a given future amount from a known present amount or vice versa.

GETTING STARTED

To access this module from the main menu, use the arrow keys to highlight the choice **Financial Mathematics** and press the ⟨**Enter**⟩ key. At this point, the Financial Mathematics Problem Menu will appear giving a choice among the seven submodules. The selection of a particular submodule is carried out using the same procedure.

NOTATION

The rest of this chapter will explain the use of different submodules by solving illustrative examples. In the following discussion, the symbols used are:

$$PV = \text{Present Value of a Cash Flow}$$
$$FV_t = \text{Future Value of a Cash Flow at Time } t$$
$$k = \text{Interest Rate}$$
$$n = \text{Time Interval in Number of Periods}$$
$$Pmt = \text{Annuity Payment}$$
$$CF_t = \text{Cash Flow at Time } t$$
$$\text{PVAN, PVAND} = \text{Present Value of an Ordinary Annuity/Annuity Due}$$
$$\text{FVAN, FVAND} = \text{Future Value of an Ordinary Annuity/Annuity Due}$$

PVIF, FVIF, PVIFA and FVIFA are the time value factors, with the subscripts indicating the interest rate and time variables.

GUIDELINES FOR DATA INPUT

All dollar amounts are entered simply as numbers. For example, $120,000 will be entered as "120000" without any commas or dollar signs. The interest rates are entered as percentages (e.g., an interest rate of 8.90 percent will be entered as "8.90" and *not* as ".089" or in its decimal form). The time variable normally will be entered as a number (of years) and so will be the number of compounding/discounting periods per year. For example, a 10-year annuity will require the user to input "10" as the term of the annuity. If the annuity payments are made quarterly, then "4" will be entered as the number of periods per year.

PRESENT VALUE OF A SINGLE CASH FLOW

The simplest application of the concept of time value of money is the determination of the present value of a future cash flow, given the appropriate discount rate. The expression for the present value can be written as:

$$PV = FV/(1 + k)^n$$

since

$$PVIF_{k,n} = 1/(1 + k)^n$$

the expression for the present value can also be written as

$$PV = FV \times PVIF_{k,n}$$

This calculation can be simple if you use the interest factor table to determine $PVIF_{k,n}$, the present value interest factor. The table cannot be used, however, when the discount rate, k, is a non-integer percentage. This submodule simplifies present value calculation a great deal.

To enter this submodule from the **Financial Mathematics** menu, highlight the choice **Present Value of Single Cash Flow** and press the ⟨**Enter**⟩ key. The data input screen will appear at this point.

Sample Problem

How much money should you deposit today in your bank account paying interest at the rate of 5.5 percent per year if you wish to have $5,000 in the account 3 years from now?

This problem can be solved by calculating the present value of the future amount, $5,000, at the discount rate of 5.5 percent.

$$
\begin{aligned}
PV &= \$5,000.00 \times PVIF_{.055,3} \\
&= \$5,000.00 \times 1/(1.055)^3 \\
&= \$4,258.07
\end{aligned}
$$

To solve the above problem using the software, enter the following data:

Cash Flow	= 5000
Annual Interest Rate	= 5.5
Year in Which the Cash Flow is Received	= 3
Number of Discounting Periods per Year	= 1

The data entry screen will appear as in Figure 2.1. After making sure that all data are entered correctly, highlight the choice **Show Results** and press ⟨**Enter**⟩. The solution screen, shown in Figure 2.2, will present the results. The

Fig. 2.1

```
┌─────────────────────────────────────────────────────────────────┐
│                                                                   │
│              Present Value of Single Cash Flow                    │
│                                                                   │
│                          Cash Flow ($):   5000.00                 │
│                                                                   │
│                 Annual Interest Rate (%):    5.50                 │
│                                                                   │
│        Year in Which the Cash Flow is Received:       3           │
│                                                                   │
│               Number of Periods in a Year:       1               │
│                                                                   │
└─────────────────────────────────────────────────────────────────┘
```

Please hit the <ENTER> key after entering data in each field

```
┌──────────────┐
│  Edit Input  │                                     Show Results
└──────────────┘
```

solution screen will show the effective interest rate, PVIF, and the present value in dollars. The effective interest rate will be different from the interest rate entered in the data entry screen only if the discounting frequency (number of periods per year) is other than one.

Sample Problem

If you have promised your alma mater an endowment of $200,000 in 25 years from now, how much money should you deposit in your bank account today to make sure that you will have the money when needed? The annual interest rate is 5.75 percent, paid monthly.

To solve this problem with a calculator, the following procedure will be used:

$$PV = \$200,000 \times PVIF_{0.004792,300}$$
$$= \$47,667.53$$

Fig. 2.2

```
┌─────────────────────────────────────────────────────────────────┐
│                                                                   │
│         Present Value of a Single Cash Flow                       │
│                                                                   │
│                               Discrete     Continuous             │
│                               Discounting  Discounting            │
│                                                                   │
│    1.  Cash Flow ($)=             5000.00    5000.00              │
│                                                                   │
│    2.  Effective Interest Rate (%)=  5.50      --                 │
│                                                                   │
│    3.  Number of Periods=              3       --                 │
│                                                                   │
│    4.  Present Value Interest Factor= 0.8516   0.8479            │
│                                                                   │
│    5.  Present Value = (1) x (4) = 4258.07   4239.47             │
│                                                                   │
└─────────────────────────────────────────────────────────────────┘
```

```
┌────────────────┐
│  Print Results │        Edit Input      New Input      Bond Menu
└────────────────┘
```

Fig. 2.3

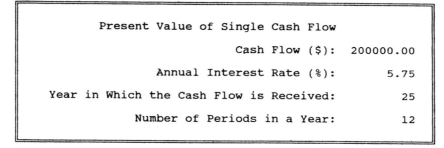

```
┌────────────────────────────────────────────────────────────────┐
│              Present Value of Single Cash Flow                  │
│                                                                 │
│                         Cash Flow ($):   200000.00             │
│                                                                 │
│                 Annual Interest Rate (%):      5.75            │
│                                                                 │
│      Year in Which the Cash Flow is Received:       25         │
│                                                                 │
│                 Number of Periods in a Year:        12         │
│                                                                 │
└────────────────────────────────────────────────────────────────┘
```

Please hit the <ENTER> key after entering data in each field

┌─────────────────┐
│   Edit Input   │   Show Results
└─────────────────┘

Enter the following data to obtain the solution using the software:

Cash Flow	= 200000
Annual Interest Rate	= 5.75
Year in which Cash Flow is Received	= 25
Number of Discounting Periods per Year	= 12

The data entry screen is shown in Figure 2.3. Highlight the choice **Show Results** and press ⟨**Enter**⟩. The solution screen will appear as shown in Figure 2.4.

The present value concept can also be used to determine the market value of zero coupon bonds, as illustrated in the following sample problem.

Fig. 2.4

```
┌────────────────────────────────────────────────────────────────┐
│            Present Value of a Single Cash Flow                  │
│                                                                 │
│                                 Discrete     Continuous         │
│                                Discounting   Discounting        │
│                                                                 │
│    1.  Cash Flow ($)=           200000.00   200000.00          │
│                                                                 │
│    2.  Effective Interest Rate (%)=   0.48       --            │
│                                                                 │
│    3.  Number of Periods=             300        --            │
│                                                                 │
│    4.  Present Value Interest Factor= 0.2318   0.2369          │
│                                                                 │
│    5.  Present Value = (1) x (4)= 47663.53   47385.55          │
│                                                                 │
└────────────────────────────────────────────────────────────────┘
```

┌─────────────────┐
│ Print Results │   Edit Input   New Input   Bond Menu
└─────────────────┘

Fig. 2.5

```
┌─────────────────────────────────────────────────────────────┐
│                                                               │
│           Present Value of Single Cash Flow                   │
│                                                               │
│                        Cash Flow ($):      1000.00            │
│                                                               │
│                Annual Interest Rate (%):      8.85            │
│                                                               │
│       Year in Which the Cash Flow is Received:      10        │
│                                                               │
│                Number of Periods in a Year:         1         │
│                                                               │
│                                                               │
└─────────────────────────────────────────────────────────────┘
```

Please hit the <ENTER> key after entering data in each field

```
┌──────────────┐
│  Edit Input  │                                Show Results
└──────────────┘
```

Sample Problem

What is the market value of a zero coupon bond with a face value of $1,000 and which matures in 10 years? The yield-to-maturity on the bond is 8.85 percent.

Market Value of the Bond = PV of $1,000 to be received in the 10th year.

$$PV = \$1000.00 \times PVIF_{.0885,10}$$
$$= \$428.27$$

Thus, the bond would sell for $428.27 in the market.

Enter the following data to determine the price of the bond using the software:

Cash Flow   = 1000

Annual Interest Rate   = 8.85

Year in Which Cash Flow is Received   = 10

Number of Discounting Periods per Year   = 1

After entering data, the screen will appear as in Figure 2.5. Highlight **Show Results** and press the ⟨**Enter**⟩ key to obtain the solution, which is presented in Figure 2.6.

FUTURE VALUE OF A SINGLE CASH FLOW

This submodule is similar in design to the previous submodule, and can be used to determine the future value of a present amount at a given interest rate. Once again, the theory is relatively simple, but applying it to practical problems can be difficult when the future value interest factor cannot be looked up in a table.

$$FV = PV \times FVIF_{k,n}$$
$$= PV \times (1 + k)^n$$

Fig. 2.6

```
┌─────────────────────────────────────────────────────────────┐
│  ┌───────────────────────────────────────────────────────┐  │
│  │         Present Value of a Single Cash Flow            │  │
│  │                                                        │  │
│  │                              Discrete    Continuous    │  │
│  │                             Discounting  Discounting   │  │
│  │                                                        │  │
│  │  1.  Cash Flow ($)=              1000.00    1000.00    │  │
│  │                                                        │  │
│  │  2.  Effective Interest Rate (%)=  8.85       --       │  │
│  │                                                        │  │
│  │  3.  Number of Periods=              10       --       │  │
│  │                                                        │  │
│  │  4.  Present Value Interest Factor= 0.4283   0.4127    │  │
│  │                                                        │  │
│  │  5.  Present Value = (1) x (4)=   428.27     412.71    │  │
│  └───────────────────────────────────────────────────────┘  │
└─────────────────────────────────────────────────────────────┘
```

┌─────────────────┐
│ Print Results   │   Edit Input   New Input   Bond Menu
└─────────────────┘

Comparing the expressions for the present value and the future value, you can see that the interest factors involved in these formulae are reciprocals of each other.

Sample Problem

Determine the amount in your $10,000 CD at the end of 4 years if the bank pays an annual interest of 8.42 percent.

$$\text{The amount in your CD} = \text{FV of } \$10,000$$
$$= \$10000.00 \times \text{FVIF}_{.0842,4}$$
$$= \$13,817.76$$

The computer solution to this problem is obtained by entering the following data in the data entry screen:

Cash Flow	= 10000
Annual Interest Rate	= 8.42
Year in Which Future Value is Needed	= 4
Number of Compounding Periods per Year	= 1

The data entry screen with the above data is shown in Figure 2.7. Highlight the choice **Show Results** on the menu bar and press the ⟨**Enter**⟩ key to get the solution screen shown in Figure 2.8.

Sample Problem

Calculate the amount accumulated in your individual retirement account (IRA), opened with $2,000 when you were 25, at your retirement at the age of 65. The bank pays interest at the annual rate of 9.00 percent, payable every quarter.

Fig. 2.7

```
┌─────────────────────────────────────────────────────────────┐
│                                                              │
│            Future Value of a Single Cash Flow                │
│                                                              │
│                         Cash Flow ($):   10000.00            │
│                                                              │
│               Annual Interest Rate (%):      8.42            │
│                                                              │
│         Year in Which Future Value is Needed:      4         │
│                                                              │
│             Number of Periods in a Year:         1           │
│                                                              │
└─────────────────────────────────────────────────────────────┘
```

Please hit the <ENTER> key after entering data in each field

┌──────────────┐
│ Edit Input │   Show Results
└──────────────┘

   The effective interest rate (i.e., the quarterly interest rate) paid by the bank is 9/4 percent or 2.25 percent. The amount will earn interest over (65 − 25) × 4, or 160 quarters.

$$\text{The amount in your IRA} = \text{FV of } \$2000$$
$$= \$2000.00 \times \text{FVIF}_{.0225,160}$$
$$= \$70{,}333.25$$

Following data are needed to obtain the software solution:

Cash Flow	= 2000
Annual Interest Rate	= 9
Year in which Future Value is Needed = 65 − 25	= 40
Number of Compounding Periods per Year	= 4

Fig. 2.8

```
┌─────────────────────────────────────────────────────────────┐
│                                                              │
│            Future Value of a Single Cash Flow                │
│                                                              │
│                               Discrete     Continuous        │
│                             Compounding   Compounding        │
│                                                              │
│   1.   Cash Flow ($)=         10000.00     10000.00          │
│                                                              │
│   2.   Effective Interest Rate (%)=   8.42      --           │
│                                                              │
│   3.   Number of Periods=             4         --           │
│                                                              │
│   4.   Future Value Interest Factor=  1.3818    1.4005       │
│                                                              │
│   5.   Future Value = (1) x (4)=  13817.76   14004.59        │
│                                                              │
└─────────────────────────────────────────────────────────────┘
```

┌──────────────────┐
│ Print Results   │   Edit Input   New Input   Bond Menu
└──────────────────┘

Fig. 2.9

```
┌─────────────────────────────────────────────────────┐
│                                                     │
│        Future Value of a Single Cash Flow           │
│                                                     │
│                       Cash Flow ($):   2000.00      │
│                                                     │
│             Annual Interest Rate (%):      9.00     │
│                                                     │
│    Year in Which Future Value is Needed:     40     │
│                                                     │
│             Number of Periods in a Year:      4     │
│                                                     │
└─────────────────────────────────────────────────────┘
```

Please hit the <ENTER> key after entering data in each field

┌──────────────┐
│ Edit Input │   Show Results
└──────────────┘

This screen is shown in Figure 2.9. The solution, which is obtained by selecting **Show Results** from the menu bar, is shown in Figure 2.10.

Sample Problem

Benjamin Franklin endowed the City of Boston $1,000 on a condition that the amount may not be spent for 100 years. If the interest rate earned by the City of Boston on this investment was 3 percent per year, calculate the amount that would accumulate at the end of the 100 years.

$$
\begin{aligned}
\text{The amount accumulated} \\
\text{at the end of 100 years} &= \text{FV} \\
&= \$1,000.00 \times \text{FVIF}_{.03,100} \\
&= \$19,218.63
\end{aligned}
$$

Fig. 2.10

```
┌─────────────────────────────────────────────────────┐
│       Future Value of a Single Cash Flow            │
│                                                     │
│                          Discrete    Continuous     │
│                         Compounding  Compounding     │
│                                                     │
│   1.  Cash Flow ($)=        2000.00    2000.00      │
│                                                     │
│   2.  Effective Interest Rate (%)=  2.25    --      │
│                                                     │
│   3.  Number of Periods=        160         --      │
│                                                     │
│   4.  Future Value Interest Factor= 35.1666  36.5982 │
│                                                     │
│   5.  Future Value = (1) x (4)=  70333.25  73196.47 │
│                                                     │
└─────────────────────────────────────────────────────┘
```

┌──────────────────┐
│ Print Results   │   Edit Input   New Input   Bond Menu
└──────────────────┘

Fig. 2.11

```
┌─────────────────────────────────────────────────────────────┐
│                                                               │
│            Future Value of a Single Cash Flow                 │
│                                                               │
│                          Cash Flow ($):   1000.00             │
│                                                               │
│                 Annual Interest Rate (%):     3.00            │
│                                                               │
│        Year in Which Future Value is Needed:     100          │
│                                                               │
│                Number of Periods in a Year:       1           │
│                                                               │
└─────────────────────────────────────────────────────────────┘
```

Please hit the <ENTER> key after entering data in each field

┌─────────────────┐
│ Edit Input   │   Show Results
└─────────────────┘

The following data are input to solve the problem using the software:

Cash Flow	= 1000
Annual Interest Rate	= 3
Year in Which Future Value is Needed	= 100
Number of Compounding Periods per Year	= 1

The data entry screen with these data entered is shown in Figure 2.11. Highlight the **Show Results** option in the menu and press the ⟨**Enter**⟩ key to obtain the solution screen shown in Figure 2.12.

Fig. 2.12

```
┌─────────────────────────────────────────────────────────────┐
│                                                               │
│              Future Value of a Single Cash Flow               │
│                                                               │
│                            Discrete      Continuous           │
│                           Compounding   Compounding           │
│                                                               │
│    1.   Cash Flow ($)=        1000.00     1000.00             │
│                                                               │
│    2.   Effective Interest Rate (%)=  3.00      --            │
│                                                               │
│    3.   Number of Periods=        100           --            │
│                                                               │
│    4.   Future Value Interest Factor= 19.2186   20.0855       │
│                                                               │
│    5.   Future Value = (1) x (4)=  19218.63   20085.54        │
│                                                               │
└─────────────────────────────────────────────────────────────┘
```

┌─────────────────┐
│ Print Results │   Edit Input   New Input   Bond **Menu**
└─────────────────┘

PRESENT VALUE OF AN ANNUITY/ANNUITY DUE

There are many practical applications of this module since loans (auto, mortgages, etc.) are usually repaid in equal payments which form an annuity. When the cash flows occur at the end of each period, the annuity is called an *ordinary annuity*. When cash flows occur at the beginning of each period, it will be defined as an *annuity due*.

The present value of an ordinary annuity is calculated as follows:

$$PVAN = Pmt \times PVIFA_{k,n}$$

where

$$PVIFA_{k,n} = \frac{1 - \dfrac{1}{(1 + k)^n}}{k}$$

The present value of an annuity due is calculated by simply multiplying the above expression by $(1 + k)$, as follows:

$$PVAND = PVAN \ X \ (1 + k)$$

To access this submodule, highlight the choice **Present Value—Annuity** on the **Financial Mathematics** menu and press the ⟨**Enter**⟩ key. This will bring up the data entry screen for annuity problems.

Sample Problem

Your car loan payments amount to $247.89 per month. If the money was borrowed for 48 months at 9.75 percent, how much was the loan amount?

$$
\begin{aligned}
\text{Loan amount} &= PVAN \\
&= \$247.89 \times PVIFA_{.0975/12,48} \\
&= \$9,820.27
\end{aligned}
$$

Enter the following data on the data entry screen to get the solution to this problem:

Annuity Payment	= 247.89
Annual Interest Rate	= 9.75
Term of the Annuity	= 4
Number of Payments per Year	= 12

This screen is shown in Figure 2.13. Highlight **Show Results** and press the ⟨**Enter**⟩ key to get the solution screen shown in Figure 2.14.

Sample Problem

Your parents have just learned that the college you will be attending costs $15,000 per year for the next four years. The first payment is due at the end of the current year. How much money should they deposit in a bank account

Fig. 2.13

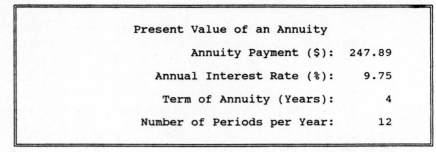

```
                    Present Value of an Annuity

                        Annuity Payment ($):   247.89

                    Annual Interest Rate (%):     9.75

                      Term of Annuity (Years):      4

                 Number of Periods per Year:       12
```

Please hit the <ENTER> key after entering data in each field

| Edit Input | Show Results

earning 5.75 percent so that your educational expenses over the next four years are taken care of?

This problem can be solved as follows:

Amount Required in the bank account = PV

$$= \$15{,}000.00 \times \text{PVIFA}_{.0575,4}$$

$$= \$52{,}275.52$$

To find the solution using the software, enter the following data:

Annuity Payment   = 15000
Annual Interest Rate   = 5.75
Term of the Annuity   = 4
Number of Payments per Year = 1

Fig. 2.14

```
                    Present Value of an Annuity

          1.  Annuity Payment ($)=                    247.89

          2.  Effective Interest Rate (%)=              0.81

          3.  Number of Payments=                         48

          4.  Pre. Val. Int. Factor of Annuity=      39.6154

          5.  Present Value = (1) X (4) =            9820.27

          6.  Present Value of Annuity Due =         9900.06
```

| Print Results | Edit Input   New Input   Bond Menu

Fig. 2.15

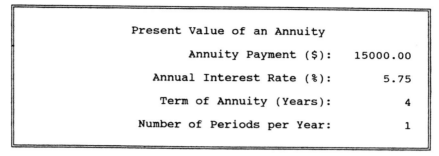

```
          Present Value of an Annuity

              Annuity Payment ($):      15000.00

         Annual Interest Rate (%):          5.75

          Term of Annuity (Years):             4

         Number of Periods per Year:           1
```

Please hit the <ENTER> key after entering data in each field

Edit Input   Show Results

This screen is shown in Figure 2.15. Highlight **Show Results** and press the ⟨**Enter**⟩ key to get the solution screen shown in Figure 2.16.

Sample Problem

Your uncle is retiring at the age of 65. He has determined that to live comfortably he will need a monthly income of $2,500. He expects to live for 30 more years. If his investments yield 9 percent, how much money does he need to invest to meet his retirement needs?

The following procedure can be used to determine the answer:

$$\text{Amount Needed} = \$2,500.00 \times \text{PVIFA}_{.09/12, 30\text{X}12}$$
$$= \$310,704.66$$

Fig. 2.16

```
              Present Value of an Annuity

     1.  Annuity Payment ($)=               15000.00

     2.  Effective Interest Rate (%)=           5.75

     3.  Number of Payments=                       4

     4.  Pre. Val. Int. Factor of Annuity=    3.4850

     5.  Present Value = (1) X (4) =        52275.52

     6.  Present Value of Annuity Due =     55281.36
```

Print Results   Edit Input   New Input   Bond **Menu**

Fig. 2.17

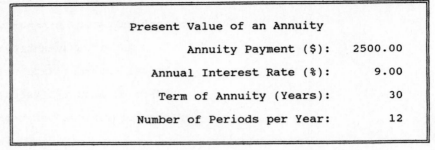

```
                    Present Value of an Annuity

                     Annuity Payment ($):      2500.00

                  Annual Interest Rate (%):        9.00

                  Term of Annuity (Years):           30

              Number of Periods per Year:           12
```

Please hit the <ENTER> key after entering data in each field

Edit Input   Show Results

The following data are entered to get the software solution:

Annuity Payment   = 2500
Annual Interest Rate   = 9
Term of the Annuity   = 30
Number of Payments per Year = 12

This screen is shown in Figure 2.17. Highlight **Show Results** and press the ⟨**Enter**⟩ key to get the solution screen shown in Figure 2.18.

Fig. 2.18

```
                    Present Value of an Annuity

          1.   Annuity Payment ($)=                 2500.00

          2.   Effective Interest Rate (%)=            0.75

          3.   Number of Payments=                      360

          4.   Pre. Val. Int. Factor of Annuity=   124.2819

          5.   Present Value = (1) X (4) =        310704.66

          6.   Present Value of Annuity Due =     313034.95
```

Print Results   Edit Input   New Input   Bond Menu

FUTURE VALUE OF AN ORDINARY ANNUITY/ANNUITY DUE

This module also can be useful in many day-to-day, practical applications. The future value of an ordinary annuity is calculated as follows:

$$\text{FVAN} = Pmt \times \text{FVIFA}_{k,n}$$

where

$$\text{FVIFA}_{k,n} = \frac{(1 + k)^n - 1}{k}$$

The future value of an annuity due is calculated by simply multiplying the above expression by $(1 + k)$, as follows:

$$\text{FVAND} = \text{FVAN} \times (1 + k)$$

To access this submodule, highlight the choice **Future Value—Annuity** on the **Financial Mathematics** menu and press the ⟨**Enter**⟩ key. This will bring up the data entry screen for annuity problems.

Sample Problem

Your financial planner has advised you to deposit $250.00 per month in your retirement account (401k). If the account earns an 8 percent annual interest, calculate how much money will be available for your retirement 25 years from now.

The amount in the retirement account $= \$250.00 \times \text{FVIFA}_{.08/12,\ 25 \times 12}$
$$= \$237,756.60$$

Enter the following data to obtain the computer solution:

Annuity Payment $= 250$
Annual Interest Rate $= 8$
Term of the Annuity $= 25$
Number of Payments per Year $= 12$

This screen is shown in Figure 2.19. Highlight **Show Results** and press the ⟨**Enter**⟩ key to get the solution screen shown in Figure 2.20.

Sample Problem

Ms. Sarika Smith, age 25, has decided to deposit $2,000 per year in her IRA account until her retirement at the age of 65. If the IRA account earns 8 percent interest, how much money will have accumulated in her account at age 65?

The amount in her IRA account can be calculated as follows:

Amount in IRA account $= \$2,000 \times \text{FVIFA}_{.08,30}$
$$= \$226,566.42$$

Fig. 2.19

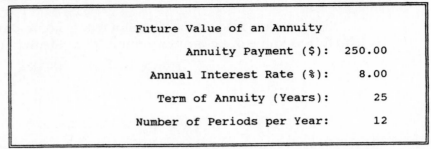

```
┌──────────────────────────────────────────────────┐
│                                                  │
│              Future Value of an Annuity          │
│                                                  │
│              Annuity Payment ($):   250.00       │
│                                                  │
│         Annual Interest Rate (%):     8.00       │
│                                                  │
│           Term of Annuity (Years):      25       │
│                                                  │
│       Number of Periods per Year:       12       │
│                                                  │
└──────────────────────────────────────────────────┘
```

Please hit the <ENTER> key after entering data in each field

┌──────────────────┐
│   Edit Input   │   Show Results
└──────────────────┘

The software solution can be obtained by entering the following data:

Annuity Payment   = 2000
Annual Interest Rate   = 8
Term of the Annuity   = 30   =   (65 − 25)
Number of Payments per Year   = 1

This screen is shown in Figure 2.21. Highlight **Show Results** and press the ⟨**Enter**⟩ key to get the solution screen shown in Figure 2.22.

Sample Problem

Joe and Ruth Schwartz have rented out their Daytona Beach holiday apartment at $700 a month, payable at the beginning of each month. The rent

Fig. 2.20

```
┌──────────────────────────────────────────────────┐
│                                                  │
│            Future Value of an Annuity            │
│                                                  │
│    1.   Annuity Payment ($)=              250.00 │
│                                                  │
│    2.   Effective Interest Rate (%)=        0.67 │
│                                                  │
│    3.   Number of Payments=                  300 │
│                                                  │
│    4.   Fut. Val. Int. Factor of Annuity=  951.0264 │
│                                                  │
│    5.   Future Value = (1) X (4) =      237756.60 │
│                                                  │
│    6.   Future Value of Annuity Due =   239341.64 │
│                                                  │
└──────────────────────────────────────────────────┘
```

┌──────────────────┐
│ Print Results   │   Edit Input   New Input   Bond Menu
└──────────────────┘

Fig. 2.21

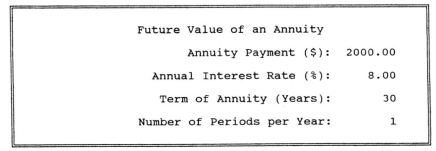

```
                 Future Value of an Annuity

              Annuity Payment ($):  2000.00

           Annual Interest Rate (%):    8.00

            Term of Annuity (Years):      30

          Number of Periods per Year:      1
```

Please hit the <ENTER> key after entering data in each field

Edit Input   Show Results

is directly deposited in a bank account paying an annual interest of 6 percent. Calculate the amount in this bank account at the end of five years.

This problem deals with an annuity where cash flows are received at the beginning of each period instead of at the end. This type of cash flow is known as an annuity due.

$$\text{The amount in the bank} = \$700 \times \text{FVIFA}_{.06/12, 5 \times 12} \times (1 + .06/12)$$
$$= \$49{,}083.22$$

Enter the following data to obtain the solution:

Annuity Payment　　　　　　　　$= 700$

Annual Interest Rate　　　　　　$= 6$

Term of the Annuity　　　　　　$= 5$

Number of Payments per Year　$= 12$

Fig. 2.22

```
                 Future Value of an Annuity

    1.  Annuity Payment ($)=                2000.00

    2.  Effective Interest Rate (%)=           8.00

    3.  Number of Payments=                      30

    4.  Fut. Val. Int. Factor of Annuity=   113.2832

    5.  Future Value = (1) X (4) =         226566.60

    6.  Future Value of Annuity Due =      244691.74
```

Print Results   Edit Input   New Input   Bond Menu

Fig. 2.23

```
┌─────────────────────────────────────────────────────────┐
│                                                         │
│             Future Value of an Annuity                  │
│                                                         │
│             Annuity Payment ($):      700.00            │
│                                                         │
│          Annual Interest Rate (%):      6.00            │
│                                                         │
│           Term of Annuity (Years):         5            │
│                                                         │
│          Number of Periods per Year:       1            │
│                                                         │
│                                                         │
└─────────────────────────────────────────────────────────┘
```

Please hit the <ENTER> key after entering data in each field

```
┌─────────────────┐
│  Edit Input     │                              Show Results
└─────────────────┘
```

This screen is shown in Figure 2.23. Highlight **Show Results** and press the ⟨**Enter**⟩ key to get the solution screen shown in Figure 2.24.

PRESENT/FUTURE VALUE OF AN IRREGULAR CASH FLOW STREAM

Most cash flows in real-world applications are not in the form of annuities. To determine the present or future value of irregular cash flows, students must calculate the present value or future value of each cash flow separately and then add all results together. This can get very tedious if the number of cash flows is large. This submodule will eliminate the repetitive calculations and obtain a solution to such problems in seconds.

The present value of an irregular cash flow stream will be determined using the following equation:

$$PV = \sum_{t=1}^{n} \frac{CF_t}{(1 + k)^t}$$

Fig. 2.24

```
┌─────────────────────────────────────────────────────────┐
│                                                         │
│              Future Value of an Annuity                 │
│                                                         │
│     1.  Annuity Payment ($)=                  700.00    │
│                                                         │
│     2.  Effective Interest Rate (%)=            0.50    │
│                                                         │
│     3.  Number of Payments=                       60    │
│                                                         │
│     4.  Fut. Val. Int. Factor of Annuity=    69.7700    │
│                                                         │
│     5.  Future Value = (1) X (4) =          48839.02    │
│                                                         │
│     6.  Future Value of Annuity Due =       49083.22    │
│                                                         │
└─────────────────────────────────────────────────────────┘
```

```
┌─────────────────┐
│  Print Results  │      Edit Input       New Input       Bond Menu
└─────────────────┘
```

The future value of an irregular cash flow stream will be determined using the following equation:

$$FV = \sum_{t=1}^{n} CF_t (1 + k)^{n-t}$$

To access this submodule, highlight the choice **Pres./Fut. Val. of Irregular Cash Flow** and press the ⟨**Enter**⟩ key. This will bring up the data entry screen which allows entry of up to 30 cash flows. The first two sample problems calculate the present values of irregular cash flows, while the remaining sample problem calculates the future value of an irregular stream of cash flow.

Sample Problem

Calculate the market value of a variable coupon bond which pays interest at the rate of 10 percent for the first five years, and 11 percent for the next five years. The face value of this bond is $1,000 and it is priced to yield 12 percent.

Unlike ordinary bond problems, coupon payments from this bond vary over the 10-year life of the bond. Problems like this one cannot be solved in one step using the annuity factor. This problem can be solved as follows:

Market Price of the Bond = PV of Future Cash Flows =
$100 × PVIFA$_{.12,5}$ + $110 × PVIFA$_{.12,5}$ × PVIF$_{.12,5}$ + $1,000 × PVIF$_{.12,10}$
= $907.47

The software solution to this problem can be obtained by entering the following:

Interest Rate	= 12
Number of Cash Flows	= 10
Cash Flow for Years 1–5	= 100
Cash Flow for Years 6–9	= 110
Cash Flow for Year 10	= 110 + 1000 = 1110

This screen is shown in Figure 2.25. Since the problem calls for the calculation of the present value of the cash flow, highlight the choice **Calculate Pres. Value** and press the ⟨**Enter**⟩ key to get the solution screen shown in Figure 2.26.

Sample Problem

Lynn Utang is planning for her three-year-old daughter's college education. She expects that in 15 years, tuition for a four-year college education will be $30,000, $31,000, $32,000, and $33,000, respectively. How much money should Lynn set aside in an investment earning 10 percent a year to meet her daughter's tuition expenses?

Amount Needed = PV of Future Cash Flows
= $30,000 × PVIF$_{.10,15}$ + $31,000 × PVIF$_{.10,16}$
$32,000 × PVIF$_{.10,17}$ + $33,000 × PVIF$_{.10,18}$
= $26,193.90

Fig. 2.25

```
┌──────────────────────────────────────────────────────────────────────────┐
│          Present Value of Irregular Stream of Cash Flows                   │
│                                                                            │
│      Interest Rate (%):  12.00        Number of Cash Flows:  10            │
│                                                                            │
│   Period   Cash Flow      Period   Cash Flow      Period   Cash Flow       │
│     1       100.00          11                      21                     │
│     2       100.00          12                      22                     │
│     3       100.00          13                      23                     │
│     4       100.00          14                      24                     │
│     5       100.00          15                      25                     │
│     6       110.00          16                      26                     │
│     7       110.00          17                      27                     │
│     8       110.00          18                      28                     │
│     9       110.00          19                      29                     │
│    10      1110.00          20                      30                     │
│                                                                            │
└──────────────────────────────────────────────────────────────────────────┘
```

Please hit the <ENTER> key after entering data in each field

```
┌──────────────┐
│  Edit Input  │                                    Show Results
└──────────────┘
```

Enter the following data to obtain the solution using the software:

Interest Rate	= 10
Number of Cash Flows	= 18 (Start counting from Yr. 1)
Cash Flow for Years 1–14	= 0
Cash Flow for Year 15	= 30000
Cash Flow for Year 16	= 31000
Cash Flow for Year 17	= 32000
Cash Flow for Year 18	= 33000

This data input screen is shown in Figure 2.27. Highlight **Calculate Pres. Value** and press the ⟨**Enter**⟩ key to get the solution screen shown in Figure 2.28.

Fig. 2.26

```
┌──────────────────────────────────────────────────────────┐
│        Present Value of Irregular Cash Flow Stream        │
│                                                           │
│    1.   Interest Rate (%)=              12.00             │
│                                                           │
│    2.   Number of Payments=               10             │
│                                                           │
│    3.   Present Value =                 907.45            │
│                                                           │
└──────────────────────────────────────────────────────────┘
```

```
┌───────────────┐
│ Print Results │     Edit Input      New Input      Bond Menu
└───────────────┘
```

Fig. 2.27

```
┌─────────────────────────────────────────────────────────────────────┐
│            Present Value of Irregular Stream of Cash Flows            │
│                                                                       │
│      Interest Rate (%):  10.00        Number of Cash Flows:  18       │
│                                                                       │
│   Period    Cash Flow     Period    Cash Flow     Period   Cash Flow  │
│      1        0.00          11        0.00           21                │
│      2        0.00          12        0.00           22                │
│      3        0.00          13        0.00           23                │
│      4        0.00          14        0.00           24                │
│      5        0.00          15      30000.00         25                │
│      6        0.00          16      31000.00         26                │
│      7        0.00          17      32000.00         27                │
│      8        0.00          18      33000.00         28                │
│      9        0.00          19                       29                │
│     10        0.00          20                       30                │
│                                                                       │
└─────────────────────────────────────────────────────────────────────┘
```

Please hit the <ENTER> key after entering data in each field

```
┌───────────────┐
│  Edit Input   │                              Show Results
└───────────────┘
```

Sample Problem

Omega Airways is planning to deposit $5 million, $6 million, $7 million, and $8 million at the end of each of the next four years in an account earning 9 percent. This account will be used to retire the company's outstanding bond issue. How many dollars worth of bonds will the company be able to retire at the end of four years?

This problem requires students to calculate the future value of the uneven cash flows. The solution is:

$$\text{Dollar Amount of Bonds Retired} = \text{FV of Uneven Cash Flow}$$
$$= \$5 \text{ million} \times \text{FVIF}_{.09,3} + \$6 \text{ million} \times \text{FVIF}_{.09,2}$$
$$+ \$7 \text{ million} \times \text{FVIF}_{.09,1} + \$8 \text{ million}$$
$$= \$29.23 \text{ million}$$

Fig. 2.28

```
┌─────────────────────────────────────────────────────────────┐
│                                                             │
│       Present Value of Irregular Cash Flow Stream           │
│                                                             │
│    1.   Interest Rate (%)=                  10.00           │
│                                                             │
│    2.   Number of Payments=                   18           │
│                                                             │
│    3.   Present Value =                  26914.63           │
│                                                             │
└─────────────────────────────────────────────────────────────┘
```

```
┌─────────────────┐
│  Print Results  │      Edit Input       New Input       Bond Menu
└─────────────────┘
```

Fig. 2.29

```
┌─────────────────────────────────────────────────────────────────┐
│          Future Value of Irregular Stream of Cash Flows           │
│                                                                   │
│      Interest Rate (%):  9.00        Number of Cash Flows:   4     │
│                                                                   │
│    Period    Cash Flow     Period   Cash Flow     Period   Cash Flow │
│      1         5.00          11                     21            │
│      2         6.00          12                     22            │
│      3         7.00          13                     23            │
│      4         8.00          14                     24            │
│      5                       15                     25            │
│      6                       16                     26            │
│      7                       17                     27            │
│      8                       18                     28            │
│      9                       19                     29            │
│     10                       20                     30            │
└─────────────────────────────────────────────────────────────────┘
```

Please hit the <ENTER> key after entering data in each field

```
┌─────────────┐
│ Edit Input  │                              Show Results
└─────────────┘
```

The computer solution needs the following data:

Interest Rate	= 9
Number of Cash Flows	= 4
Cash Flow for Year 1	= 5
Cash Flow for Year 2	= 6
Cash Flow for Year 3	= 7
Cash Flow for Year 4	= 8

After data entry, the data input screen will appear as shown in Figure 2.29. This time the future value of the cash flow is needed. Therefore, highlight **Calculate Future Value** and press the ⟨**Enter**⟩ key to get the solution screen shown in Figure 2.30. Since the dollar amounts entered were in units of millions of dollars, the solution should also be interpreted in millions of dollars.

Fig. 2.30

```
┌──────────────────────────────────────────────────────────┐
│        Future Value of Irregular Cash Flow Stream          │
│                                                            │
│   1.   Interest Rate (%)=            9.00                   │
│                                                            │
│   2.   Number of Payments=              4                  │
│                                                            │
│   3.   Future Value =               29.23                  │
└──────────────────────────────────────────────────────────┘
```

```
┌───────────────┐
│ Print Results │        Edit Input      New Input      Bond Menu
└───────────────┘
```

ANNUITY PAYMENT NEEDED FOR PRESENT/FUTURE VALUE

Many financial transactions in every individual's life require a good understanding of how to determine the amount of payment needed to pay off a loan or to accumulate a future sum. This submodule simplifies such calculations.

If the present value is provided, then the annuity payment can be calculated using the following equation:

$$Pmt = \frac{PV}{PVIFA_{k,n}} = \frac{PV}{\dfrac{1 - \dfrac{1}{(1 + k)^n}}{k}}$$

Similarly, the annuity payment needed to accumulate a future sum is calculated as follows:

$$Pmt = \frac{FV}{FVIFA_{k,n}} = \frac{FV}{\dfrac{(1 + k)^n - 1}{k}}$$

To access the submodule, highlight the selection in the **Financial Mathematics** menu and press the ⟨**enter**⟩ key. This will bring up the data entry screen for the submodule.

Sample Problem

You have decided to borrow $12,500 for your new car from a bank charging a 13.59 percent annual interest. The loan has to be paid back in four years, making 48 monthly payments. Calculate the monthly payment on this loan.

$$\text{The loan payment} = \$12,500/PVIFA_{k,n}$$
$$= \$339.02$$

To solve the problem, enter the following data in the input screen:

Present/Future Amount	= 12500
Annual Interest Rate	= 13.59
Term of the Annuity	= 4
Number of Payments per Year	= 12

The screen will appear as in Figure 2.31 after data entry. Since the problem has provided the present value for which annuity payment needs to be calculated, highlight **Payment for Pres. Val.** and press the ⟨**Enter**⟩ key to get the solution screen shown in Figure 2.32.

Sample Problem

Your parents have decided to finance your college education by taking out a home equity loan of $25,000 payable in 10 years at an annual interest rate of 11.75 percent. Calculate the monthly payment needed to pay back the loan amount.

Fig. 2.31

```
┌─────────────────────────────────────────────────┐
│                                                 │
│        Annuity Payment for Present/Future Value  │
│                                                 │
│          Present/Future Amount ($):  12500.00   │
│                                                 │
│           Annual Interest Rate (%):     13.59   │
│                                                 │
│          Term of the Annuity (Years):       4   │
│                                                 │
│          Number of Payments per Year:      12   │
│                                                 │
│                                                 │
└─────────────────────────────────────────────────┘
```

Please hit the <ENTER> key after entering data in each field

┌──────────────┐
│ Edit Input   │   Payment for Pres. Val.   Payment for Future Val.
└──────────────┘

The Payment for the Home Equity Loan = $25{,}000/\text{PVIFA}_{k,n}$
= \$355.07

The following data need to be entered to find the monthly payment for the home equity loan:

Present/Future Amount   = 25000
Annual Interest Rate   = 11.75
Term of the Annuity   = 10
Number of Payments per Year = 12

The screen is shown in Figure 2.33 after data entry. Once again, since the problem has provided the present value for which annuity payment needs to be calculated, highlight **Payment for Pres. Val.** and press the ⟨**Enter**⟩ key to get the solution screen shown in Figure 2.34.

Fig. 2.32

```
┌─────────────────────────────────────────────────┐
│         Annuity Payment for Present Value        │
│  1. Future   Value =                 12500.00   │
│  2. Interest Rate per Period =           1.133  │
│  3. PV Interest Factor of an Annuity =  36.8710 │
│  4. Annuity Payment =                  339.02   │
└─────────────────────────────────────────────────┘
```

┌──────────────┐
│ Print Results│   Edit Input   New Input   FM Menu
└──────────────┘

Fig. 2.33

```
┌─────────────────────────────────────────────────────┐
│                                                       │
│       Annuity Payment for Present/Future Value        │
│                                                       │
│         Present/Future Amount ($):   25000.00         │
│                                                       │
│           Annual Interest Rate (%):     11.75         │
│                                                       │
│        Term of the Annuity (Years):        10         │
│                                                       │
│         Number of Payments per Year:       12         │
│                                                       │
│                                                       │
└─────────────────────────────────────────────────────┘
```

Please hit the <ENTER> key after entering data in each field

┌──────────────┐
│ Edit Input │   Payment for Pres. Val.   Payment for Future Val.
└──────────────┘

Sample Problem

You have decided to travel to Europe after your graduation two years from now. You estimate that this trip will cost you $3,500 at the time. Determine the amount you will need to set aside every month in your bank account earning an interest of 5.75 percent per year so that you will have the money needed for the trip.

$$\text{The Monthly Deposit Needed} = 3{,}500/\text{FVIFA}_{k,n}$$
$$= \$137.96$$

The following data are needed to find the solution using the software:

Present/Future Amount	= 3500
Annual Interest Rate	= 5.75
Term of the Annuity	= 2
Number of Payments per Year	= 12

Fig. 2.34

```
┌─────────────────────────────────────────────────────┐
│          Annuity Payment for Present Value            │
│                                                       │
│   1. Future  Value =                     25000.00     │
│                                                       │
│   2. Interest Rate per Period =              0.979    │
│                                                       │
│   3. PV Interest Factor of an Annuity =     70.4087   │
│                                                       │
│   4. Annuity Payment =                      355.07    │
└─────────────────────────────────────────────────────┘
```

┌────────────────┐
│ Print Results │   Edit Input   New Input   FM Menu
└────────────────┘

Fig. 2.35

```
┌──────────────────────────────────────────────────────┐
│  ┌──────────────────────────────────────────────┐    │
│  │                                              │    │
│  │     Annuity Payment for Present/Future Value │    │
│  │        Present/Future Amount ($):   3500.00  │    │
│  │         Annual Interest Rate (%):      5.75  │    │
│  │        Term of the Annuity (Years):       2  │    │
│  │        Number of Payments per Year:      12  │    │
│  │                                              │    │
│  └──────────────────────────────────────────────┘    │
└──────────────────────────────────────────────────────┘
```

Please hit the <ENTER> key after entering data in each field

```
┌──────────────┐
│  Edit Input  │     Payment for Pres. Val.   Payment for Future Val.
└──────────────┘
```

The screen is shown in Figure 2.35 after data entry. This problem provides the future amount for which the annuity payment needs to be calculated. Therefore, highlight **Payment for Fut. Val.** and press the ⟨**Enter**⟩ key to get the solution screen shown in Figure 2.36.

Sample Problem

Determine the annual payment needed to accumulate $500,000 in your retirement account 30 years from now. The money will be invested to earn an interest of 9.00 percent per year.

$$\text{The Annual Payment} = 500{,}000/\text{FVIFA}_{k,n}$$
$$= \$3{,}668.18$$

Fig. 2.36

```
┌──────────────────────────────────────────────────────┐
│           Annuity Payment for Future Value            │
│   1. Future   Value =                    3500.00      │
│   2. Interest Rate per Period =             0.479     │
│   3. FV Interest Factor of an Annuity =    25.3697    │
│   4. Annuity Payment =                    137.96      │
└──────────────────────────────────────────────────────┘
```

```
┌──────────────────┐
│  Print Results   │     Edit Input     New Input     FM Menu
└──────────────────┘
```

Fig. 2.37

```
┌──────────────────────────────────────────────────────┐
│                                                        │
│        Annuity Payment for Present/Future Value        │
│            Present/Future Amount ($): 500000.00        │
│            Annual Interest Rate (%):      9.00         │
│          Term of the Annuity (Years):       30         │
│          Number of Payments per Year:        1         │
│                                                        │
└──────────────────────────────────────────────────────┘
```

Please hit the <ENTER> key after entering data in each field

┌─────────────┐
│ Edit Input │   Payment for Pres. Val.   Payment for Future Val.
└─────────────┘

The input data for this problem are:

Present/Future Amount   = 500000
Annual Interest Rate   = 9
Term of the Annuity   = 30   (Years)
Number of Payments per Year   = 1

The screen is shown in Figure 2.37 after data entry. This problem also provides future amount for which the annuity payment needs to be calculated. Therefore, highlight **Payment for Fut. Val.** and press the ⟨**Enter**⟩ key to get the solution screen shown in Figure 2.38.

Fig. 2.38

```
┌──────────────────────────────────────────────────────┐
│           Annuity Payment for Future Value            │
│                                                        │
│   1. Future   Value =                  500000.00       │
│                                                        │
│   2. Interest Rate per Period =            9.000       │
│                                                        │
│   3. FV Interest Factor of an Annuity =  136.3075      │
│                                                        │
│   4. Annuity Payment =                   3668.18       │
└──────────────────────────────────────────────────────┘
```

┌───────────────┐
│ Print Results │   Edit Input   New Input   FM Menu
└───────────────┘

PERIOD REQUIRED TO ACHIEVE PRESENT/FUTURE VALUE

This submodule will prove useful when the student is confronted with a problem to estimate the time required to achieve a future value from a given present value at a known interest rate. The calculation procedure is based on the basic time value of money equation:

$$FV = PV \times FVIF_{k,n}$$

In the above equation, all the variables are known except n, the time period. The equation can be solved for n as follows:

$$
\begin{aligned}
FV &= PV \times FVIF_{k,n} \\
&= PV \times (1 + k)^n \\
(1 + k)^n &= FV/PV
\end{aligned}
$$

Taking natural logarithms of both sides,

$$n \times \ln(1 + k) = \ln(FV/PV)$$

and, finally

$$n = \frac{\ln\left(\dfrac{FV}{PV}\right)}{\ln(1 + k)}$$

To access the submodule, highlight the selection in the **Financial Mathematics** menu and press the ⟨**Enter**⟩ key. This will bring up the data entry screen for the submodule.

Sample Problem

As a simple exercise, we will use this submodule to prove the well-known rule of 72. This rule states that the product of the percentage interest rate and the time it takes to double an amount at that interest rate is approximately 72. The rule can be proven for one specific case as follows:

Since the future value is twice the present amount regardless of the present amount, $FVIF_{k,n}$ is always equal to 2.000. To determine the number of years it takes to double a beginning amount at 8 percent annual interest rate, we apply the equation:

$$n = \ln(2.000)/\ln(1 + .08) = 0.6932/0.07696 = 9.007 \text{ years.}$$

Thus, the solution is 9 years. By the rule of 72, the time taken to double an amount at 8 percent annual rate should be 72/8, or 9 years.

The following data are needed to find the solution using the software:

Present Cash Flow   = 1000

Future Cash Flow   = 2000

Annual Interest Rate   = 8

Number of Periods per Year   = 1   (Annual interest rate)

Fig. 2.39

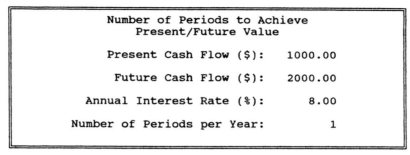

Please hit the <ENTER> key after entering data in each field

Edit Input   Show Results

The screen is shown in Figure 2.39 after data entry. Highlight **Show Results** in the menu bar and press the ⟨**Enter**⟩ key to get the solution screen shown in Figure 2.40.

This concludes the discussion of illustrative examples on the topic of financial mathematics. To access the next module, highlight the choice **FM Menu** on the menu bar on the solution screen and press the ⟨**Enter**⟩ key. This will take you back to the main menu of the submodule. Again, highlight the choice **Investment Problems Menu** and press the ⟨**Enter**⟩ key. The control will be returned to the main menu, from where you may select any other module.

Fig. 2.40

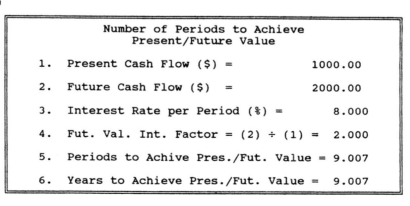

Print Results   Edit Input   New Input   FM Menu

3 *Bond Analysis*

In any course on investments or security analysis and portfolio management, a significant amount of class time is devoted to the analysis of fixed-income securities, namely, bonds and preferred stocks. The bond analysis module in **Investment Problem Solver** is designed to eliminate tedious and repetitive calculations, such as working out the present values of annuities and single cash flows.

The bond analysis module includes the following five submodules:

1. Bond Price—Interest Date
2. Bond Price—Non-interest Date
3. Yield-to-Maturity
4. Yield-to-First Call
5. Duration

These five submodules are designed to tackle a wide variety of problems involving different kinds of bonds. One major exception is the topic of convertible bonds. Because of their special features, convertible bonds are grouped together with options in the module for hybrid securities.

Submodules 1 and 2 deal with bond price calculations. The first submodule calculates the price of a bond on an interest date (i.e., immediately after the most recent interest payment has been made). Bond pricing on a date other than the interest date is slightly more complicated and this topic is dealt with in submodule number 2.

Submodule number 3 calculates the yield-to-maturity of a bond to a high degree of precision using a trial and error procedure. Because of the algorithm used in seeking the solution the process usually converges in less than 10 iterations regardless of the type of bond. Submodule 4 is similar and solves for the yield-to-first call for bonds with a call provision.

Submodule number 5 is used to determine the Macaulay's duration of a bond. Calculation of the duration of a bond with a term to maturity of ten years with semi-annual interest payments would require a student to work out 21 rows of numbers and add them together. This submodule makes the calculation of duration a matter of seconds.

The subsequent discussion in this chapter is devoted to illustrative examples. A wide variety of problems in bond analysis are selected from some of the most popular textbooks on investment and security analysis.

GETTING STARTED

To access the **Bond Analysis** module, enter the command **IPS** (or the appropriate batch file name) after booting up the computer. At this point, the **Investment Problems Menu** screen will appear. Use the space bar or the arrow keys to move the highlight bar up or down the menu. To make the selection, highlight the choice **Bond Analysis** and press the ⟨**Enter**⟩ key. This action will bring up the next menu on the screen which lists the five submodules in the bond analysis module. The selection of the desired submodule can be made using the same procedure as above.

NOTATION

The remaining part of this chapter will be devoted to discussing several sample problems illustrating the use of each of the five submodules. In the discussion that follows, the following symbols are used:

P = Market price of the bond
I = Coupon interest payment
i = Coupon interest rate
M = Face value of the bond
k = Yield-to-maturity (YTM) of the bond
n = The term to maturity in years
P_c = Call price of the bond

Various formulae involving the summation sign will use t as the index variable for summation. Also, the terms PVIF and PVIFA with appropriate subscripts refer to the present value interest factor and the present value interest factor for an annuity, respectively.

BOND PRICE—INTEREST DATE

This submodule calculates the price of a bond by discounting the interest payments and face value of the bond at the market yield. The formula for calculating the bond price is:

$$P = \sum_{t=1}^{n} \frac{I}{(1 + k)^t} + \frac{M}{(1 + k)^n}$$

Using the familiar present value factors, the above equation translates into:

$$P = I \cdot \text{PVIFA}_{k,n} + M \cdot \text{PVIF}_{k,n}$$

To enter the **Bond Price—Interest Date** submodule, highlight that choice in the menu and press the ⟨**Enter**⟩ key. The input screen entitled **Bond Data Screen** will appear. The bond variables are entered at this point to obtain a solution.

Sample Problem

Calculate the price of a $1,000 face value zero coupon bond with a 10-year maturity. The yield-to-maturity on this bond is 8 percent.

This is a fairly simple problem. The solution is:

$$\text{Bond Price} = 1,000 \times \text{PVIF}_{.08,10}$$
$$= \$463.20$$

Enter the following data in the data entry screen of this submodule to determine the bond price using the software:

Face Value	= 1000
Coupon Rate	= 0
Number of Coupon Payments Remaining	= 10
Yield-to-Maturity	= 8
Number of Coupon Payments per Year	= 1

Upon entering these data, the input screen will appear as shown in Figure 3.1. A menu bar will appear at the bottom of the screen giving the user an opportunity to edit the input data if any input errors are detected, or to see the results (**Show Results**). Highlight the choice **Show Results** using the right arrow key or the space bar and press ⟨**Enter**⟩. The solution procedure screen shown in Figure 3.2 will appear.

Fig. 3.1

```
                         Bond Data

                   Face Value ($):   1000.00

                  Coupon Rate (%):       0

    Number of Coupon Pmts Remaining:     10

             Yield to Maturity (%):       8

     Number of Coupon Pmts per Year:      1
```

Please hit the <ENTER> key after entering data in each field

| Edit Input | Show Results

Fig. 3.2

```
┌──────────────────────────────────────────────────────┐
│                 Bond Price Calculation                │
│                                                        │
│   1.   Number of Coupon Payments=              10      │
│                                                        │
│   2.   Discount Rate Used(%)=                8.00      │
│                                                        │
│   3.   Present Value of Coupons($)=          0.00      │
│                                                        │
│   4.   Present Value of the Principal($)=  463.19      │
│                                                        │
│   5.   The Sum of (3) & (4) Equals                     │
│        the Price of the Bond($)=           463.19      │
│                                                        │
└──────────────────────────────────────────────────────┘
```

┌─────────────────┐
│ Print Results   │   Edit Input   New Input   Bond Menu
└─────────────────┘

The bottom of the screen shows the menu bar giving the student choices for different actions: **Print Results**, **Edit Input**, **New Input**, or return to the **Bond Menu**. To solve more bond pricing problems, use the arrow keys or the space bar to highlight **New Input**, and press the ⟨**Enter**⟩ key. The **Bond Data** screen will appear once again.

Sample Problem

Calculate the market price of a $1,000 par, 21-year bonds, with a 7 percent coupon rate. The yield-to-maturity on these bonds is 5 percent and the bonds are not callable. Assume annual compounding.

A student solving this problem without the aid of a computer program will go through the following process:

$$\text{Coupon Interest Amount} = .07 \times \$1,000.00$$
$$= \$70.00$$
$$\text{Term to maturity} = 21 \text{ years}$$
$$\text{Bond Price} = \$70 \times \text{PVIFA}_{.07,\,21} + \$1,000 \times \text{PVIF}_{.07,\,21}$$
$$= \$70 \times 12.8212 + \$1,000 \times 0.3589$$
$$= \$897.48 + \$358.90$$
$$= \$1,256.38$$

The input data for this problem will be as follows:

Face Value	= 1000
Coupon Rate	= 7
Number of Coupon Payments Remaining	= 21
Yield-to-Maturity	= 5
Number of Coupon Payments per Year	= 1

Fig. 3.3

```
┌─────────────────────────────────────────────────────────┐
│                                                         │
│                    Bond Data                            │
│                                                         │
│                   Face Value ($): 1000.00               │
│                                                         │
│                  Coupon Rate (%):    7.00               │
│                                                         │
│      Number of ˌCoupon Pmts Remaining:     21           │
│                                                         │
│             Yield to Maturity (%):    5.00              │
│                                                         │
│      Number of Coupon Pmts per Year:      1             │
│                                                         │
│                                                         │
└─────────────────────────────────────────────────────────┘
```

Please hit the <ENTER> key after entering data in each field

```
┌──────────────┐
│  Edit Input  │                              Show Results
└──────────────┘
```

Enter these data in the data entry screen which should appear as in Figure 3.3. Highlight the choice **Show Results** using the right arrow key or the space bar and press ⟨**Enter**⟩. The solution procedure screen shown in Figure 3.4 will appear.

Sample Problem

Two bonds have par values of $1,000—one is a 5 percent, 15-year bond priced to yield 8 percent, and the other is a 7.5 percent 20-year bond priced to yield 6 percent. Which of these two has the lower price? (Hint: Use the program to calculate each bond price separately).*

Fig. 3.4

```
┌──────────────────────────────────────────────────────────────┐
│                                                              │
│                  Bond Price Calculation                      │
│                                                              │
│   1.   Number of Coupon Payments=              21            │
│                                                              │
│   2.   Discount Rate Used(%)=                5.000           │
│                                                              │
│   3.   Present Value of Coupons($)=         897.48           │
│                                                              │
│   4.   Present Value of the Principal($)=   358.94           │
│                                                              │
│   5.   The Sum of (3) & (4) Equals                           │
│          the Price of the Bond($)=         1256.42           │
│                                                              │
└──────────────────────────────────────────────────────────────┘
```

```
┌────────────────┐
│ Print Results  │      Edit Input      New Input      Bond Menu
└────────────────┘
```

*Problem from *Fundamentals of Investments* by Lawrence J. Gitman and Michael D. Joehnk. © 1990 by Lawrence J. Gitman and Michael D. Joehnk. Reprinted with permission from HarperCollins Publishers.

Using the bond price formula, the two solutions to the problem will be calculated as:

$$P_1 = \$50 \times \text{PVIFA}_{.08,15} + \$1{,}000 \times \text{PVIF}_{.08,15}$$
$$= \$50 \times 8.559 + \$1{,}000 \times 0.315$$
$$= \$427.95 + 315.00$$
$$= \$742.95$$

and,
$$P_2 = \$75 \times \text{PVIFA}_{.06,20} + \$1{,}000 \times \text{PVIF}_{.06,20}$$
$$= \$75 \times 11.470 + \$1{,}000 \times 0.312$$
$$= \$860.25 + \$312$$
$$= \$1{,}172.25$$

The input data for the first bond are:

Face Value	= 1000
Coupon Rate	= 5
Number of Coupon Payments Remaining	= 15
Yield-to-Maturity	= 8
Number of Coupon Payments per Year	= 1

Once the above data are entered, the **Bond Data** screen will appear as in Figure 3.5. Highlighting **Show Results** options and pressing the ⟨**Enter**⟩ key will bring up The **solution procedure** screen as seen in Figure 3.6.

To solve for the second bond price, move the highlight bar to **New Input** on the menu at the bottom of the screen. Press the ⟨**Enter**⟩ key and the **Bond Data** screen will reappear. The input data for this bond are:

Face Value	= 1000
Coupon Rate	= 7.5
Number of Coupon Payments Remaining	= 20
Yield-to-Maturity	= 6
Number of Coupon Payments per Year	= 1

Fig. 3.5

```
                           Bond Data

                       Face Value ($):   1000.00

                      Coupon Rate (%):      5.00

        Number of Coupon Pmts Remaining:      15

                 Yield to Maturity (%):      8.00

        Number of Coupon Pmts per Year:       1
```

Please hit the <ENTER> key after entering data in each field

```
Edit Input                                      Show Results
```

Fig. 3.6

```
┌─────────────────────────────────────────────────────────┐
│                                                         │
│              Bond Price Calculation                     │
│                                                         │
│   1.   Number of Coupon Payments=              15       │
│                                                         │
│   2.   Discount Rate Used(%)=               8.000       │
│                                                         │
│   3.   Present Value of Coupons($)=        427.97       │
│                                                         │
│   4.   Present Value of the Principal($)=  315.24       │
│                                                         │
│   5.   The Sum of (3) & (4) Equals                      │
│           the Price of the Bond($)=        743.22       │
│                                                         │
└─────────────────────────────────────────────────────────┘
```

```
┌──────────────────┐
│  Print Results   │      Edit Input      New Input      Bond Menu
└──────────────────┘
```

The data input screen and the solution screen are shown in Figures 3.7 and 3.8, respectively. Now the student can compare the price of the first bond with the price of the second bond to answer the question.

Highlight **New Input** on the menu at the bottom of the screen and press ⟨**Enter**⟩ to continue to the next problem.

Sample Problem

What is the price of a $1,000 face value bond with a coupon rate of 14 percent if the bond has an effective annual yield-to-maturity of 21 percent and 15 years until maturity? Assume that the bond pays semi-annual coupons and that the next coupon payment arrives 6 months from now.*

The solution procedure to this problem, using the bond price formula is as follows:

$$P = \$70 \times \text{PVIFA}_{.105,30} + \$1,000 \times \text{PVIF}_{.105,30}$$

Fig. 3.7

```
┌─────────────────────────────────────────────────────────┐
│                                                         │
│                     Bond Data                           │
│                                                         │
│                   Face Value ($): 1000.00               │
│                                                         │
│                  Coupon Rate (%):    7.50               │
│                                                         │
│       Number of Coupon Pmts Remaining:      6           │
│                                                         │
│               Yield to Maturity (%):     6.00           │
│                                                         │
│       Number of Coupon Pmts per Year:       1           │
│                                                         │
└─────────────────────────────────────────────────────────┘
```

Please hit the <ENTER> key after entering data in each field

```
┌──────────────────┐
│   Edit Input     │                        Show Results
└──────────────────┘
```

*Problem from *Investments* by Zvi Bodie, Alex Kane, and Alan J. Marcus. © 1989 by Richard D. Irwin. Reprinted with permission from Richard D. Irwin.

Fig. 3.8

```
┌─────────────────────────────────────────────────────────┐
│  ┌───────────────────────────────────────────────────┐  │
│  │              Bond Price Calculation               │  │
│  │                                                   │  │
│  │   1.  Number of Coupon Payments=            20    │  │
│  │                                                   │  │
│  │   2.  Discount Rate Used(%)=             6.000    │  │
│  │                                                   │  │
│  │   3.  Present Value of Coupons($)=      860.24    │  │
│  │                                                   │  │
│  │   4.  Present Value of the Principal($)= 311.80   │  │
│  │                                                   │  │
│  │   5.  The Sum of (3) & (4) Equals                 │  │
│  │          the Price of the Bond($)=     1172.05    │  │
│  └───────────────────────────────────────────────────┘  │
└─────────────────────────────────────────────────────────┘
```

┌───────────────────┐
│ Print Results   │   Edit Input   New Input   Bond Menu
└───────────────────┘

At this point, you must calculate the respective present value factors because the above factors are not to be found in any table. Thus, the student must know and be able to apply the formulae for both the present value interest factor and the present value interest factor of an annuity. This adds to the time spent on a problem like this.

$$P = \$70 \times 9.04744 + \$1,000 \times 0.05001$$
$$= \$633.32 + \$50.01$$
$$= \$683.33$$

The input data to solve this problem using the software are:

Face Value	= 1000
Coupon Rate	= 14
Number of Coupon Payments Remaining	= 15 × 2 = 30
Yield-to-Maturity	= 21
Number of Coupon Payments per Year	= 2

After entering these data in the **Bond Data** screen, it will appear as in Figure 3.9. The solution screen can be brought up by highlighting the **Show Results** option on the menu bar and pressing the ⟨**Enter**⟩ key. It is shown in Figure 3.10.

Sample Problem

Calculate the price of a zero coupon bond with a face value of $1,000 and maturing in 15 years. The yield-to-maturity of this bond is 9.56 percent.

This problem can be solved as follows:

$$P = M \times \text{PVIF}_{.0956,15}$$
$$= \$1,000 \times 0.2542$$
$$= \$254.20$$

Fig. 3.9

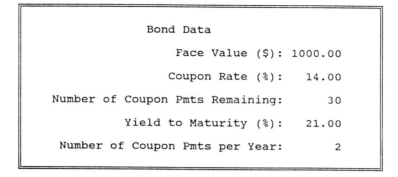

```
                    Bond Data

                    Face Value ($): 1000.00

                   Coupon Rate (%):    14.00

    Number of Coupon Pmts Remaining:      30

          Yield to Maturity (%):      21.00

    Number of Coupon Pmts per Year:       2
```

Please hit the <ENTER> key after entering data in each field

Edit Input   Show Results

To solve this problem using the software, bring up the **Bond Data** screen and enter the following data:

Face Value	= 1000
Coupon Rate	= 0
Number of Coupon Payments Remaining	= 15
Yield-to-Maturity	= 9.56
Number of Coupon Payments Per Year	= 1

After data input, the **Bond Data** screen should appear as in Figure 3.11. Highlight the choice **Show Results** and press the ⟨**Enter**⟩ key to bring up the solution screen, which is shown in Figure 3.12.

Fig. 3.10

```
             Bond Price Calculation

    1.  Number of Coupon Payments=            30

    2.  Discount Rate Used(%)=            10.500

    3.  Present Value of Coupons($)=     633.32

    4.  Present Value of the Principal($)=  50.02

    5.  The Sum of (3) & (4) Equals
            the Price of the Bond($)=    683.34
```

Print Results   Edit Input   New Input   Bond Menu

Fig. 3.11

```
┌─────────────────────────────────────────────────────────┐
│ ┌─────────────────────────────────────────────────────┐ │
│ │                     Bond Data                       │ │
│ │                                                     │ │
│ │             Face Value ($):  1000.00                │ │
│ │                                                     │ │
│ │            Coupon Rate (%):     0.00                │ │
│ │                                                     │ │
│ │  Number of Coupon Pmts Remaining:       15          │ │
│ │                                                     │ │
│ │          Yield to Maturity (%):     9.56            │ │
│ │                                                     │ │
│ │  Number of Coupon Pmts per Year:        1           │ │
│ └─────────────────────────────────────────────────────┘ │
└─────────────────────────────────────────────────────────┘
```

Please hit the <ENTER> key after entering data in each field

| Edit Input | Show Results

Fig. 3.12

```
┌─────────────────────────────────────────────────────────┐
│ ┌─────────────────────────────────────────────────────┐ │
│ │               Bond Price Calculation                │ │
│ │                                                     │ │
│ │  1.  Number of Coupon Payments=            15       │ │
│ │                                                     │ │
│ │  2.  Discount Rate Used(%)=              9.560      │ │
│ │                                                     │ │
│ │  3.  Present Value of Coupons($)=         0.00      │ │
│ │                                                     │ │
│ │  4.  Present Value of the Principal($)=  254.23     │ │
│ │                                                     │ │
│ │  5.  The Sum of (3) & (4) Equals                    │ │
│ │          the Price of the Bond($)=       254.23     │ │
│ └─────────────────────────────────────────────────────┘ │
└─────────────────────────────────────────────────────────┘
```

| Print Results | Edit Input   New Input   Bond Menu

BOND PRICE—NON-INTEREST DATE

This submodule differs from the previous submodule in one respect: When the bond price is to be calculated at a date other than those on which interest payments are made, the calculation becomes more involved. The following algorithm is used to calculate the price of the bond on a non-interest date:

1. Determine the price of the bond at the **next** interest payment date using the standard bond valuation procedure.
2. Add the coupon payment to be received at the next interest date.
3. Discount this sum to its present value.
4. Adjust the computed value for the accumulated interest amount.

A user may enter this submodule directly from the main menu, using the following steps:

1. Highlight the choice **Bond Analysis** in the main menu using the arrow keys or the space bar.
2. Press the ⟨**Enter**⟩ key to bring up the bond menu.
3. Highlight **Bond Price—Non-Interest Date** choice.
4. Press the ⟨**Enter**⟩ key to bring up the data input screen.

The use of this submodule will be illustrated with a number of sample problems.

Sample Problem

A bond has a par value of $1,000 and a coupon rate of 9 percent. There are 13 semi-annual coupon payments remaining on the bond and 40 days to the next coupon payment. If the yield-to-maturity is 11 percent, what is the price of the bond?

This problem can be solved without the help of a computer program in the following manner:

$$
\begin{aligned}
\text{Discount Rate} &= 11/2 = 5.5\% \\
\text{Face Value} &= \$1,000 \\
\text{Coupon Payment} &= \$90 \text{ per year or } \$45 \text{ semi-annually} \\
P &= \text{Bond price after the next interest payment} \\
&= \$45 \times \text{PVIFA}_{.055,12} + \$1,000 \times \text{PVIF}_{.055,12} \\
&= \$45 \times 8.6185 + \$1,000 \times 0.526 \\
&= \$387.83 + \$526.00 \\
&= \$913.83
\end{aligned}
$$

Next, add the coupon payment to this price:

$$
\begin{aligned}
P + I &= \$913.83 + \$45.00 \\
&= \$958.83
\end{aligned}
$$

The Present Value of this price as of today is

$$
\begin{aligned}
\text{PV} &= \$958.83 \times \text{PVIF}_{.055,40/180} \\
&= \$947.49
\end{aligned}
$$

Finally, calculate the accumulated interest and subtract it from the above price.

$$
\begin{aligned}
\text{Accumulated interest} &= (180 - 40)/180 \times \$45 = \$35.00 \\
\text{Price of the bond} &= \$947.49 - \$35.00 = \$912.49
\end{aligned}
$$

To solve this problem using the software, bring up the **Bond Data** screen using the procedure described above. The input variables for the bond are as follows:

Face Value	= 1000
Coupon Rate	= 9

Number of Coupon Payments Remaining   = 13
Yield-to-Maturity   = 11
Number of Coupon Payments per Year   = 2
Number of Days to Next Interest Payment   = 40

After entering the above data, the **Bond Data** screen will appear as in Figure 3.13. Highlight the choice **Show Results** and press the ⟨**Enter**⟩ key to bring up the solution. It is shown in Figure 3.14.

Move the highlight bar to **New Input** and press the ⟨**Enter**⟩ key to continue to the next problem.

Sample Problem

A bond paying semi-annual interest has a life of 12 years, 6 months, and 27 days. The bond has a coupon rate of 5 percent and a par value of $1,000. The yield-to-maturity is 9.5 percent. What is the price of the bond?
  The solution for this problem is:

$$P = \$25 \times \text{PVIFA}_{.0475,24} + \$1,000 \times \text{PVIF}_{.0475,24}$$
$$= \$681.84$$
$$P + I = \$706.84$$
$$PV = \$701.19$$
$$\text{Acc. Interest} = (180 - 27) \times 25 = \$21.25$$
$$\text{Price of the bond} = \$679.94$$

The computer solution for this problem is obtained by entering the following data:

Face Value   = 1000
Coupon Rate   = 5

Fig. 3.13

```
                    Bond Data

                  Face Value ($):   1000.00

                 Coupon Rate (%):      9.0

   Number of Coupon Pmts Remaining:     13

            Yield to Maturity (%):    11.00

   Number of Coupon Pmts per Year:       2

       Days to Next Interest Date:      40

```

Please hit the <ENTER> key after entering data in each field

┌─────────────┐
│ Edit Input │   Show Results
└─────────────┘

Fig. 3.14

```
                    Bond Price Calculation

     1.   Number of Coupon Payments=                13

     2.   Discount Rate Used(%)=                   5.500

     3.   Present Value of Coupons($)=             427.78

     4.   Present Value of the Principal($)=       519.85

     5.   Accrued Interest Amounts($)=              35.14

     6.   The Sum (3)+(4)-(5) Equals
          the Price of the Bond($)=                912.49
```

```
Print Results        Edit Input        New Input        Bond Menu
```

Number of Coupon Payments Remaining	=	25
Yield-to-Maturity	=	9.5
Number of Coupon Payments per Year	=	2
Number of Days to Next Interest Payment	=	27

Enter this information on the bond and the **Bond Data** screen will appear as seen in Figure 3.15. The solution procedure screen will appear as shown in Figure 3.16.

Move the highlight bar to **New Input** and press ⟨**Enter**⟩ for the next problem.

Fig. 3.15

```
                         Bond Data

                   Face Value ($):   1000.00

                   Coupon Rate (%):      5.0

      Number of Coupon Pmts Remaining:    25

               Yield to Maturity (%):   9.50

      Number of Coupon Pmts per Year:     2

          Days to Next Interest Date:     27
```

```
Please hit the <ENTER> key after entering data in each field
```

```
Edit Input                              Show Results
```

Fig. 3.16

```
┌──────────────────────────────────────────────────────────┐
│                  Bond Price Calculation                   │
│                                                            │
│     1.   Number of Coupon Payments=            25          │
│                                                            │
│     2.   Discount Rate Used(%)=               4.750        │
│                                                            │
│     3.   Present Value of Coupons($)=         375.92       │
│                                                            │
│     4.   Present Value of the Principal($)=   326.08       │
│                                                            │
│     5.   Accrued Interest Amounts($)=          21.30       │
│                                                            │
│     6.   The Sum (3)+(4)-(5) Equals                        │
│          the Price of the Bond($)=            680.70       │
│                                                            │
└──────────────────────────────────────────────────────────┘
```

Print Results	Edit Input	New Input	Bond Menu

Sample Problem

A firm issued a $1,000 face value, 20-year bond, with a 9 percent coupon rate 8 years and six and a half months ago. If the current interest rate is 10 percent, at what price would the bond sell?

Once again, this problem can be solved in the following steps:

First, calculate the bond price at the next interest date, assuming annual interest payments:

$$P = \$90.00 \times \text{PVIFA}_{.10,11} + \$1,000.00 \times \text{PVIF}_{.10,11}$$
$$= \$90.00 \times 6.4950 + \$1,000.00 \times 0.3505$$
$$= \$935.05$$

Next, one coupon payment is added to the price:

$$P = \$935.05 + \$90.00 = \$1,025.05$$

This price is discounted back to today,

$$PV = \$1,025.05 \times 1/(1.10)^{165/365}$$
$$= \$981.82$$

Finally, the accumulated interest amount for six and a half months is deducted from the above price:

$$P = \$981.82 - 90 \times 200/365$$
$$= \$932.50$$

To solve this problem using the software, the following data need to be entered:

Face Value	= 1000
Coupon Rate	= 9

Number of Coupon Payments Remaining = 20 − 8   = 12

Yield-to-Maturity   = 10

Number of Coupon Payments per Year   = 1

Number of Days to Next Interest Payment   = 165

Enter these values and the **Bond Data** screen will appear as in Figure 3.17. Highlight the choice **Show Results** and press ⟨**Enter**⟩ and the Solution Procedure screen will appear as shown in Figure 3.18.

Fig. 3.17

```
                           Bond Data

                      Face Value ($):   1000.00

                     Coupon Rate (%):      9.00

         Number of Coupon Pmts Remaining:    12

                 Yield to Maturity (%):    10.00

         Number of Coupon Pmts per Year:       1

             Days to Next Interest Date:     165
```

Please hit the <ENTER> key after entering data in each field

Edit Input   Show Results

Fig. 3.18

```
                  Bond Price Calculation

        1.  Number of Coupon Payments=          12

        2.  Discount Rate Used(%)=              10.000

        3.  Present Value of Coupons($)=        646.11

        4.  Present Value of the Principal($)=  335.71

        5.  Accrued Interest Amounts($)=         49.32

        6.  The Sum (3)+(4)-(5) Equals
            the Price of the Bond($)=           932.51
```

Print Results   Edit Input   New Input   Bond Menu

YIELD-TO-MATURITY

The yield-to-maturity is the rate of return that would be earned on the bond if it is purchased today and held to maturity. It is assumed that all of the bond coupons are reinvested at the yield-to-maturity rate. If this is not true, the actual yield-to-maturity will not be the same as the bond's calculated yield-to-maturity.

To calculate the yield-to-maturity, k, the following bond price equation has to be solved for k, given the price of the bond.

$$P = \sum_{t=1}^{t=n} \frac{I}{(1+k)^t} + \frac{M}{(1+k)^n}$$

Since the above equation cannot be solved analytically for k, a trial and error procedure has to be used to determine the value of k which will yield the price of the bond.

To bring up the yield-to-maturity submodule, the following steps are taken:

1. If you are in the main menu, then highlight the choice **Bond Analysis** and press the ⟨**Enter**⟩ key.

2. In the Bond Analysis menu, highlight the choice **Yield To Maturity** and press the ⟨**Enter**⟩ key.

This will bring up the data input screen.

Sample Problem

Ordway Corp. has a 14 percent debenture bond outstanding that matures in twenty years. The bond is callable in five years at 114. It currently sells for 105. Calculate the yield-to-maturity for the bond.*

This problem can be solved without the help of a computer program in the following manner:

$$P = I \times \text{PVIFA}_{k,n} + M \times \text{PVIF}_{k,n}$$
$$1050 = 140 \times \text{PVIFA}_{k,20} + 1,000 \times \text{PVIF}_{k,20}$$

At this point, different values for k will be tried until the price of $1,050 is obtained from the above equation.

Trial 1: $k = 13$
$RHS = 140 \times 7.025 + 1,000 \times 0.087 = 1,070.50 > 1,050$
Trial 2: $k = 13.5$
$RHS = 140 \times 6.8189 + 1,000 \times 0.07945 = 1,034.09 < 1,050$

You can now estimate the approximate yield-to-maturity using interpolation between 13 percent and 13.5 percent or continue the trial and error process by choosing a number between 13 and 13.5.

---

*Problem from *Security Analysis and Portfolio Management* by Donald E. Fischer and Ronald J. Jordan. © 1991 by Prentice Hall, Inc. Reprinted with permission from Prentice Hall, Inc.

Interpolation solution is 13.50 − (1,050.00 − 1,034.09)/(1,070.50 − 1,034.09) × 0.50 = 13.28%.

The input data for this problem are:

Market Price	= 1050
Face value	= 1000
Coupon Rate	= 14
Term-to-Maturity	= 20
Number of Coupon Payments per Year	= 1

When these variables are entered on the **Bond Data** screen, it will appear as in Figure 3.19. Highlight the choice **Show Results** and press the ⟨**Enter**⟩ key and the **Bond Yield Calculation** screen with the trial and error solution is presented. This screen is shown in Figure 3.20.

Use the right or left arrow to move the highlight bar to **New Input** and press the ⟨**Enter**⟩ key to bring up the data input screen once again.

Sample Problem

An investor purchases a bond for $900 with a 7 percent coupon that matures in five years. Find the yield-to-maturity, assuming annual payments.*

The trial and error solution to this problem can be found by first estimating the bond price at 9 percent.

$$P = \$70 \times \text{PVIFA}_{.09,5} + \$1,000.00 \times \text{PVIF}_{.09,5}$$
$$= \$922.18$$

Fig. 3.19

```
                        Bond Data

                Market Price ($):     1050.00

                  Face Value ($):     1000.00

                 Coupon Rate (%):       14.00

            Term to Maturity (YRS):     20.00

    Number of Coupon Pmts per Year:        1
```

Please hit the <ENTER> key after entering data in each field

```
Edit Input
```
                                        Show Results

*Problem from *Investments* by Frank K. Reilly. © 1986 by CBS College Publishing. Reprinted with permission from The Dryden Press.

Fig. 3.20

```
                              Bond Yield Calculation

     Market Price=  1050.00       Face Value=         1000.00

     Coupon Rate(%)=      14.00   Term to Maturity (Yrs)=   20.00

     TRIAL #          YIELD (GUESS)        BOND PRICE     MARKET VALUE

     1                  19.0000              744.96         1050.00
     2                  13.0198             1068.78         1050.00
     3                  13.3665             1043.54         1050.00
     4                  13.2777             1049.90         1050.00
     5                  13.2764             1050,00         1050.00
     6                  13.2764             1050.00         1050.00



              The Yield to Maturity =      13.276 percent.
```

```
     ┌─────────────────┐
     │  Print Results  │     Edit Input    New Input    Bond Menu
     └─────────────────┘
```

Next, the price will be calculated at 10 percent:

$$P = \$886.26$$

Finally, the approximate yield to maturity will be determined by interpolation:

$$YTM = 10 - (900 - 886.26)/(922.18 - 886.26)$$
$$= 9.62\%$$

The computer solution to this problem can be obtained by entering the following data:

Market Price	= 900
Face value	= 1000
Coupon Rate	= 7
Term-to-Maturity	= 5
Number of Coupon Payments per Year	= 1

After data entry, the input screen will appear as in Figure 3.21. Press the ⟨**Enter**⟩ key after highlighting the appropriate choice and the **Bond Yield Calculation** screen will appear. This screen is shown in Figure 3.22. Move the highlight bar to **New Input** and press ⟨**Enter**⟩ to do more bond problems.

Sample Problem

A 25-year, zero coupon bond was recently being quoted at 11-5/8. Find the yield-to-maturity of this issue, given that the bond has a par value of $1,000.* The solution to this problem is rather easy to find, as this is a zero coupon

*Problem from *Fundamentals of Investments* by Lawrence J. Gitman and Michael D. Joehnk. © 1990 by Lawrence J. Gitman and Michael D. Joehnk. Reprinted with permission from HarperCollins Publishers.

Fig. 3.21

```
┌──────────────────────────────────────────────────────────────┐
│                         Bond Data                             │
│                                                               │
│              Market Price ($):        900.00                  │
│                                                               │
│               Face Value ($):        1000.00                  │
│                                                               │
│              Coupon Rate (%):           7.00                  │
│                                                               │
│         Term to Maturity (YRS):         5.00                  │
│                                                               │
│   Number of Coupon Pmts per Year:          1                  │
│                                                               │
└──────────────────────────────────────────────────────────────┘
```

Please hit the <ENTER> key after entering data in each field

┌──────────────┐
│ Edit Input │   Show Results
└──────────────┘

bond. The market price of this bond is $11.625 \times 100 = \$116.25$. We can write the following equation for the price of this bond:

$$P = \$1,000.00 \times \text{PVIF}_{x,25}$$

where x is the yield-to-maturity. Thus, we can calculate the value of the present value interest factor as

$$\text{PVIF} = 116.25/1,000 = .11625 = (1 + y)^{-25}$$

Solving for y, we can find the yield-to-maturity to be 8.99%.

Fig. 3.22

                      Bond Yield Calculation

Market Price= 900.00   Face Value=   1000.00

Coupon Rate(%)=   7.00   Term to Maturity (Yrs)=   5.00

TRIAL #	YIELD (GUESS)	BOND PRICE	MARKET VALUE
1	12.0000	819.76	900.00
2	9.7741	894.23	900.00
3	9.6016	900.37	900.00
4	9.6119	900.00	900.00
5	9.6119	900.00	900.00

The Yield to Maturity =   9.612 percent.

┌──────────────────┐
│ Print Results   │   Edit Input   New Input   Bond Menu
└──────────────────┘

The following data need to be entered to find the solution using the software:

Market Price	= 116.25
Face value	= 1000
Coupon Rate	= 0
Term-to-Maturity	= 25
Number of Coupon Payments per Year	= 1

Enter the required data on the **Bond Data** screen. The screen would appear as in Figure 3.23 once these data are entered. Press the ⟨**Enter**⟩ key after highlighting **Show Results** and the **Bond Yield Calculation Screen** will appear as shown in Figure 3.24. Further bond calculations can done by highlighting **New Input** and pressing the ⟨**Enter**⟩ key.

Sample Problem

A 7 percent coupon bond is currently selling for $1,100 in the market. The remaining life of the bond is 15 years. Calculate the yield-to-maturity of the bond.

Since the bond is selling at a premium, the first trial will assume the yield-to-maturity at 6 percent.

$$P = \$70.00 \times \text{PVIFA}_{.06,15} + \$1,000 \times \text{PVIF}_{.06,15}$$
$$= \$1,097.15$$

The bond price calculated above is very close to $1,100.00, the market price of the bond. Thus, the approximate yield-to-maturity of this bond is 6 percent.

The data for the computer solution of the problem are:

Market Price	= 1100
Face value	= 1000

Fig. 3.23

```
                        Bond Data

                Market Price ($):        116.25

                Face Value ($):         1000.00

               Coupon Rate (%):            0.00

         Term to Maturity (YRS):          25.00

    Number of Coupon Pmts per Year:           1


    Please hit the <ENTER> key after entering data in each field


      Edit Input                              Show Results
```

Fig. 3.24

```
                        Bond Yield Calculation

    Market Price=   116.25          Face Value=        1000.00

    Coupon Rate(%)=    0.00      Term to Maturity (Yrs)=   25.00

        TRIAL #        YIELD (GUESS)        BOND PRICE     MARKET VALUE

        1              5.0000               295.30         116.25
        2              6.2704               218.62         116.25
        3              7,9664               147.16         116.25
        4              8.6999               124.24         116.25
        5              8.9557               117.15         116.25
        6              8.9883               116.28         116.25
        7              8.9894               116.25         116.25
        8              8.9894               116.25         116.25


            The Yield to Maturity =    8.989 percent.
```

```
    | Print Results |    Edit Input      New Input      Bond Menu
```

Coupon Rate	= 7
Term-to-Maturity	= 15
Number of Coupon Payments per Year	= 1

Enter these data on the **Bond Data** screen. The screen should appear as in Figure 3.25. Highlight **New Input** and press the ⟨**Enter**⟩ key and the Bond Yield Calculation screen will appear shown in Figure 3.26.

Fig. 3.25

```
    +-----------------------------------------------------+
    |                                                     |
    |                    Bond Data                        |
    |              Market Price ($):    1100.00           |
    |                                                     |
    |               Face Value ($):     1000.00           |
    |                                                     |
    |              Coupon Rate (%):        7.00           |
    |                                                     |
    |         Term to Maturity (YRS):     15.00           |
    |                                                     |
    |     Number of Coupon Pmts per Year:     1           |
    |                                                     |
    +-----------------------------------------------------+
```

```
    Please hit the <ENTER> key after entering data in each field

    | Edit Input |                          Show Results
```

Fig. 3.26

```
                        Bond Yield Calculation

    Market Price=  1100.00      Face Value=         1000.00

    Coupon Rate(%)=    7.00      Term to Maturity (Yrs)=   15.00

    TRIAL #        YIELD (GUESS)        BOND PRICE    MARKET VALUE

    1                 12.0000            659.46        1100.00
    2                  5.5318           1147.07        1100.00
    3                  6.1561           1081.13        1100.00
    4                  5.9774           1099.46        1100.00
    5                  5.9722           1100.01        1100.00
    6                  5.9722           1100.00        1100.00
    7                  5.9722           1100.00        1100.00

                   The Yield to Maturity =        5.972 percent.
```

Print Results	Edit Input	New Input	Bond Menu

This section is now complete. Move the highlight bar to **Bond Menu** and press ⟨**Enter**⟩ to bring up the bond analysis menu.

YIELD-TO-FIRST CALL

Some bonds are issued with a special provision, the call provision, so that the issuer has an option to retire the bonds long before they reach maturity. For example, bonds issued in the early 1980s were generally issued with a call provision, because these bonds carried very high coupons. The issuers, therefore, foresaw the need to redeem the bonds before maturity and issue new bonds at a lower rate within the next few years. A call issued long before the maturity invariably hurts the investor, because now he/she has to replace the high coupon bonds with bonds paying much lower coupons. To make a well-informed decision in the case of callable bonds, an investor has to consider both the yield-to-maturity and the yield-to-call of a bond.

The yield-to-first call will be calculated in the same manner as the yield-to-maturity. The date on which the bond first becomes callable is substituted for the maturity date and the face value plus any call penalty, which is termed the call price of the bond, is substituted for the face value. The assumption here is that the issuing firm will call the bonds back at the first opportunity. The following equation is used to calculate the yield-to-first call:

$$P = \sum_{t=1}^{T} \frac{I}{(1 + r)^t} + \frac{P_c}{(1 + r)^T}$$

where T is the period between now and the year in which the bond first becomes callable, r is the yield-to-first call, and P_c is the call price of the bond. Once again, the above equation cannot be solved analytically for r and, therefore, a trial and error procedure has to be employed to determine the value of the yield-to-first call.

To bring up the **yield to first call** submodule, the following steps are followed:

1. If you are in the main menu, then highlight the choice **Bond Analysis** and press the ⟨**Enter**⟩ key.
2. In the **Bond Analysis** menu, highlight the choice **Yield To First Call** and press the ⟨**Enter**⟩ key.

This will bring up the data input screen.

Sample Problem

A $1,000 face-value bond pays interest semi-annually based on a 12 percent coupon. Its current price is $900 and it matures in 8 years. Calculate the yield-to-call on the bond if the bond is callable in 3 years at 110 percent of face value.*

The solution procedure for this problem is similar to the one used in calculating the yield-to-maturity with one difference. In the case of the yield-to-first call problems, the cash flow at call is usually greater than $1,000.00. In this case it is $1,100.00.

$$Trial\ 1: k = 18\%$$
$$P = \$60.00 \times PVIFA_{.09,6} + \$1,100.00 \times PVIF_{.09,6}$$
$$= \$925.08$$
$$Trial\ 2: k = 20\%$$
$$P = \$882.27$$

The yield-to-first call of the bond can be determined using interpolation as follows:

$$YFC = 18 + 2 \times (900 - 882.27)/(925.08 - 882.27) = 18.82\%$$

The data required for the software solution for this problem are:

Market Price	= 900
Face Value	= 1000
Coupon Rate	= 12
Term-to-First Call	= 3
Number of Coupon Payments per Year	= 2
Call Price	= 1100

Enter the above data in the input screen. The screen shown in Figure 3.27 will appear. Highlight **Show Results** and press the ⟨**Enter**⟩ key. The **Bond Yield Calculation** screen shown in Figure 3.28 will appear.

---

*Problem from *Investments: Analysis, Selection and Management* by Edward A. Moses and John M. Cheney. © 1989 by West Publishing Company. Reprinted with permission from West Publishing Company.

Fig. 3.27

```
┌──────────────────────────────────────────────────────────────┐
│                          Bond Data                             │
│                Market Price ($):      900.00                   │
│                 Face Value ($):      1000.00                   │
│                Coupon Rate (%):        12.00                   │
│        Term to First Call (YRS):        3.00                   │
│    Number of Coupon Pmts per Year:         2                   │
│                Call Price ($):      1100.00                     │
└──────────────────────────────────────────────────────────────┘
```

Please hit the <ENTER> key after entering data in each field

```
┌─────────────┐
│ Edit Input  │                                      Show Results
└─────────────┘
```

The following choices are now available: **Print Screen, Edit Input, New Input and Bond Menu**. Move the highlight to **New Input** and press the ⟨**Enter**⟩ key to solve the next problem.

Sample Problem

A bond is currently quoted at $1,100 and has a current yield of 6.36 percent. The remaining life of the bond is 15 years, but it has 3 years remaining on a deferred call feature. Calculate the yield-to-call, assuming a call premium equal to one year's interest.*

Fig. 3.28

Bond Yield Calculation

Market Price= 900.00   Call Price=   1100.00

Coupon Rate(%)=   12.00 Term to First Call (Yrs)=   3.00

TRIAL #	YIELD (GUESS)	BOND PRICE	MARKET VALUE
1	23.2100	841.94	900.00
2	20.4063	893.55	900.00
3	20.0582	900.28	900.00
4	20.0728	900.00	900.00
5	20.0727	900.00	900.00

The Yield to First Call = 20.073 percent.

```
┌─────────────────┐
│ Print Results   │   Edit Input    New Input    Bond Menu
└─────────────────┘
```

*Problem from *Investments* by Frank K. Reilly. © 1986 by CBS College Publishing. Reprinted with permission from The Dryden Press.

The coupon interest of this bond equals the current yield times the market value which is $70.00 (1,100 × 0.0636). The call price thus will be $1,000.00 + $70.00 = $1,070.00.

$$Trial\ 1: k = 6\%$$
$$P = \$1,085.48$$
$$Trial\ 2: k = 5\%$$
$$P = \$1,114.89$$

Interpolating, the yield-to-maturity is

$$YTM = 5 + (1,100.00 - 1,085.48)/(1,114.89 - 1,085.48) = 5.49\%$$

To obtain the solution for this problem using the software, enter the following data in the input screen:

Market Price	= 1100
Face Value	= 1000
Coupon Rate	= 7
Term-to-First Call	= 3
Number of Coupon Payments per Year	= 1
Call Price	= 1070

The **Bond Data** screen should appear as in Figure 3.29. Highlight **Show Results** and press the ⟨**Enter**⟩ key and the **Bond Yield Calculation** screen will appear, shown in Figure 3.30.

Sample Problem

A bond is available at a price of 102. The bond has a coupon of 15 percent and matures in 20 years. The bond is callable in 5 years at 111. What is the yield-to-call on the bond?*

$$Trial\ 1: k = 16\%$$
$$P = \$150 \times PVIFA_{.16,5} + \$1,110 \times PVIF_{.16,5}$$
$$= \$1,019.62$$

For all practical purposes, this price is close to the market value of the bond or $1020.00. Thus, the yield-to-first call is 16 percent.

Enter the following data on the **Bond Data** screen:

Market Price	= 1020
Face Value	= 1000
Coupon Rate	= 15
Term-to-First Call	= 5
Number of Coupon Payments per Year	= 1
Call Price	= 1110

*Problem from *Security Analysis and Portfolio Management* by Donald E. Fischer and Ronald J. Jordan. © 1991 by Prentice Hall, Inc. Reprinted with permission from Prentice Hall, Inc.

Fig. 3.29

```
┌─────────────────────────────────────────────────────────────┐
│                         Bond Data                           │
│                                                             │
│              Market Price ($):     1100.00                  │
│                                                             │
│                Face Value ($):     1000.00                  │
│                                                             │
│              Coupon Rate (%):         7.00                  │
│                                                             │
│      Term to First Call (YRS):        3.00                  │
│                                                             │
│   Number of Coupon Pmts per Year:        1                  │
│                                                             │
│               Call Price ($):      1070.00                  │
│                                                             │
└─────────────────────────────────────────────────────────────┘
```

Please hit the <ENTER> key after entering data in each field

┌──────────────┐
│ Edit Input │   Show Results
└──────────────┘

The **Bond Data** screen should appear as in Figure 3.31. Highlight **Show Results** and press the ⟨**Enter**⟩ key and the **Bond Yield Calculation** screen will appear, shown in Figure 3.30.

The following choices are now available: **Print Screen**, **Edit Input**, **New Input**, or **Bond Menu**. Move the highlight bar to **Bond Menu** and press ⟨**Enter**⟩. The program is now back to the Bond Analysis menu.

Fig. 3.30

```
                          Bond Yield Calculation

    Market Price=        1100.00    ·Call Price=              1070.00

    Coupon Rate (%)=        7.00  Term to First Call (Yrs)=     3.00

         TRIAL #    YIELD (GUESS)      BOND PRICE      MARKET VALUE

         1          12.0000            929.73          1100.00
         2           5.3180           1105.46          1100.00
         3           5.5255           1099.33          1100.00
         4           5.5029           1100.00          1100.00
         5           5.5028           1100.00          1100.00

         The Yield to First Call =  5.503 percent.
```

┌─────────────────┐
│ Print Results   │   Edit Input   New Input   Bond Menu
└─────────────────┘

Fig. 3.31

```
┌─────────────────────────────────────────────────────────────┐
│                         Bond Data                            │
│                                                              │
│                Market Price ($):     1020.00                 │
│                                                              │
│                 Face Value ($):      1000.00                 │
│                                                              │
│                Coupon Rate (%):        15.00                 │
│                                                              │
│           Term to First Call (YRS):     5.00                 │
│                                                              │
│      Number of Coupon Pmts per Year:       1                 │
│                                                              │
│                 Call Price ($):      1110.00                 │
│                                                              │
└─────────────────────────────────────────────────────────────┘
```

Please hit the <ENTER> key after entering data in each field

┌─────────────────┐
│   Edit Input   │   Show Results
└─────────────────┘

Fig. 3.32

Bond Yield Calculation

Market Price= 1020.00   Call Price =   1110.00

Coupon Rate (%)=   15.00   Term to First Call (Yrs)= 5.00

TRIAL #	YIELD (GUESS)	BOND PRICE	MARKET VALUE
1	20.0000	894.68	1020.00
2	16.0840	1016.76	1020.00
3	15.9801	1020.31	1020.00
4	15.9892	1020.00	1020.00
5	15.9892	1020.00	1020.00

The Yield to First Call = 15.989 percent.

┌──────────────────┐
│ Print Results   │   Edit Input   New Input   Bond Menu
└──────────────────┘

DURATION

Duration is a measure of the "average maturity" of the stream of cash flows associated with a bond. Bond analysts use different duration measures. The simplest of these is the Macaulay's duration. The following discussion uses this concept of duration.

Duration is an important variable in bond analysis because it measures the price elasticity of a bond. Thus, for small changes in interest rates, an investor can determine the change in price of a bond based on the duration of the bond. The longer the duration, the greater the price volatility of the bond for any given change in interest rates. The higher the coupon, the shorter the duration of the bond. Likewise, a zero coupon bond would have a duration equal to the yield-to-maturity.

The duration of a bond can be determined from the following equation:

$$D = \frac{\sum_{t=1}^{n} \dfrac{t \cdot CF_t}{(1 + k)^t}}{\sum_{t=1}^{n} \dfrac{CF_t}{(1 + k)^t}}$$

where CF_t is the cash flow from the bond in the period t. The formula for duration assumes that the bond in question will not be called early and that the yield curve is flat.

To bring up the duration submodule, the following steps are followed:

1. If you are in the main menu, then highlight the choice **Bond Analysis** and press the ⟨**Enter**⟩ key.

2. In the **Bond Analysis** menu, highlight the choice **Duration** and press the ⟨**Enter**⟩ key.

This will bring up the data input screen for duration problems.

Sample Problem

A bond can be acquired with a 4-year maturity. The bond has a coupon rate of 12 percent and is priced in the market at 100. What is the duration of this bond? Assume semi-annual payments.*

The calculations in the solution for duration problems without the help of the software are basically the same as seen on the computer screen. To avoid duplication, the solution procedure is not presented here.

To obtain the computer solution to the above problem, enter the following data:

Face Value	= 1000
Coupon Rate	= 12
Term-to-Maturity	= 4
Yield-to-Maturity	= 12 (Since it is a par bond)
Number of Coupons per Year	= 2

The **Bond Data** screen will appear as in Figure 3.33. Highlight **Show Results** and press the ⟨**Enter**⟩ key and the **Duration Calculation** screen will appear on the screen, as in Figure 3.34.

---

*Problem from *Security Analysis and Portfolio Management* by Donald E. Fischer and Ronald J. Jordan. © 1991 by Prentice Hall, Inc. Reprinted with permission from Prentice Hall, Inc.

Fig. 3.33

```
                            Bond Data

                    Face Value ($):   1000.00

                    Coupon Rate (%):    12.00

              Term to Maturity (Yrs):    4.00

              Yield to Maturity (%):    12.00

      Number of Coupon Pmts per Year:        2
```

Please hit the <ENTER> key after entering data in each field

Edit Input   Show Results

Move the highlight bar to **New Input** and press ⟨**Enter**⟩ to continue working problems on duration.

Sample Problem

Calculate the duration of a 3-year bond with a 7 percent coupon. The yield-to-maturity of this bond is 8 percent.

The input data for this problem are:

Face Value	= 1000
Coupon Rate	= 7
Term-to-Maturity	= 3
Yield-to-Maturity	= 8
Number of Coupon Payments per Year	= 1

Fig. 3.34

Duration Calculation

Period(T)	Cash Flow(CF)	PV of Cash Flow	T x PV of CF
1	60.00	56.60	56.60
2	60.00	53.40	106.80
3	60.00	50.38	151.13
4	60.00	47.53	190.10
5	60.00	44.84	224.18
6	60.00	42.30	253.79
7	60.00	39.90	279.32
8	1060.00	665.06	5320.46
Totals		1000.00	6582.38

Duration of the Bond is   =   6.58 periods
                             =   3.29 Years

Print Results   Edit Input   New Input   Bond Menu

Enter the required values and the **Bond Data** screen will appear as in Figure 3.35. Highlight **Show Results** and press ⟨**Enter**⟩ and the **Duration Calculation** screen will appear. This screen is shown in Figure 3.36.

Sample Problem

Find the duration of a 6 percent coupon bond making annual coupon payments if it has 3 years until maturity and has a yield-to-maturity of 6 percent.*

The input data to solve this problem are:

Face Value	= 1000
Coupon Rate	= 6
Term-to-Maturity	= 3
Yield-to-Maturity	= 6
Number of Coupon Payments per Year	= 1

Enter the bond data on the **Bond Data** screen and it will appear as in Figure 3.37. Highlight **Show Results** and press ⟨**Enter**⟩ and the **Duration Calculation** screen shown in Figure 3.38 appears.

To continue working problems, move the highlight bar to **New Input** and press ⟨**Enter**⟩.

Sample Problem

Consider a bond selling at its par value of $1,000, with three years-to-maturity and a 10 percent coupon rate (with annual interest payments). Calculate the bond's duration.*

Fig. 3.35

```
                    Bond Data

                Face Value ($):   1000.00

                Coupon Rate (%):     7.00

           Term to Maturity (Yrs):  3.00

           Yield to Maturity (%):   8.00

    Number of Coupon Pmts per Year:    1
```

Please hit the <ENTER> key after entering data in each field

```
Edit Input
```
                                    Show Results

---

*Problem from *Investments* by Zvi Bodie, Alex Kane, and Alan J. Marcus. ©1989 by Richard D. Irwin. Reprinted with permission from Richard D. Irwin.

*Problem from *Investments* by William F. Sharpe and Gordon J. Alexander. © 1990 by Prentice Hall, Inc. Reprinted with permission from Prentice Hall, Inc.

Fig. 3.36

<pre>
                        Duration Calculation

    Period(T) Cash Flow(CF)   PV of Cash Flow   T x PV of CF

        1   70.00   64.81   64.81
        2   70.00   60.01   120.03
        3   1070.00   849.40   2548.20

            Totals   974.23   2733.04

        Duration of the Bond is   =   2.81 periods
                                       =   2.81 Years
</pre>

| Print Results | Edit Input | New Input | Bond Menu |

The input data for this problem are:

Face Value	= 1000
Coupon Rate	= 10
Term-to-Maturity	= 3
Yield-to-Maturity	= 10 (Bond sells at par)
Number of Coupon Payments per Year	= 1

Enter the bond data on the **Bond Data** screen and it will appear as in Figure 3.39. Highlight **Show Results** and press ⟨**Enter**⟩ and the **Duration Calculation** screen shown in Figure 3.40 appears.

This was the last section of the **Bond Analysis** module. Move the highlight bar to **Bond Menu** and press ⟨**Enter**⟩. This returns the control of the program to the Bond Analysis Menu. Now move the highlight bar to **Main Menu** and press the ⟨**Enter**⟩ key again. The control is now returned to the **Investment Problems Menu**.

Fig. 3.37

<pre>
                        Bond Data

                 Face Value ($):   1000.00

                Coupon Rate (%):   6.00

          Term to Maturity (Yrs):   3.00

          Yield to Maturity (%):   6.00

   Number of Coupon Pmts per Year: 1
</pre>

Please hit the <ENTER> key after entering data in each field

| Edit Input | Show Results

Fig. 3.38

Duration Calculation

Period(T)	Cash Flow(CF)	PV of Cash Flow	T x PV of CF
1	60.00	56.60	56.60
2	60.00	53.40	106.80
3	1060.00	890.00	2669.99
Totals		1000.00	2833.39

Duration of the Bond is   =   2.83 periods
                                 =   2.83 Years

| Print Results | Edit Input | New Input | Bond Menu |

Fig. 3.39

.Bond Data

Face Value ($): 1000.00

Coupon Rate (%):   10.00

Term to Maturity (Yrs):   3.00

Yield to Maturity (%):   10.00

Number of Coupon Pmts per Year: 1

Please hit the <ENTER> key after entering data in each field

| Edit Input | Show Results

Fig. 3.40

Duration Calculation

Period(T)	Cash Flow(CF)	PV of Cash Flow	T x PV of CF
1	100.00	90.91	90.91
2	100.00	82.64	165.29
3	1100.00	826.45	2479.34
Totals		1000.00	2735.54

Duration of the Bond is   =   2.74 periods
                          =   2.74 Years

| Print Results | Edit Input | New Input | Bond Menu |

4 *Common Stock Analysis*

Common stock analysis is an important topic in investments analysis because of the popularity of common stock among alternative investment instruments. Students face a variety of problems in common stock analysis:

1. margin analysis;
2. calculation of holding period yield with and without margin; and
3. common stock valuation using different assumptions.

All these types of problems can be solved using the **Common Stock Analysis** module in **Investment Problem Solver**. Some related issues like the determination of the beta of a common stock and risk-return analysis of common stocks are dealt with later in the **Portfolio Theory** module.

The **Common Stock Analysis** module contains the following submodules:

1. Margin Analysis—Purchases
2. Margin Analysis—Short Sales
3. Holding Period Yield
4. Average Rate of Return
5. Constant Growth Stock Price
6. Supernormal Growth Stock Price

Submodule 1 tackles problems which involve purchase of common stock on margin. This submodule accepts data about the initial margin, the maintenance margin, and the purchase price of the stock to determine the actual margin percentage and the stock price at which the investor will receive a margin call. The solution also presents details of the investor's margin account in the form of a balance sheet. Submodule 2 performs the same tasks in the case of short sales on margin.

The third submodule handles problems which require calculation of the holding period yield for common stocks. The price data of common stock along with the dividend information are the required input. The submodule calculates the holding period yield with and without margin.

Submodule 4 can be used to calculate the average rate of return from any security. Both the arithmetic and the geometric average rate of return are presented in the solution screen.

Submodule 5 uses the Gordon Growth Model to calculate the price of a common stock which is expected to grow at a constant rate of growth for the foreseeable future.

The last submodule deals with the more complicated problems in common stock valuation where the growth rate is not constant.

GETTING STARTED

Common Stock Analysis is the third module among the five modules in the software package. Return to the **Investments Problems Menu** screen which is also referred to as the main menu. Using the arrow keys, move the highlight bar down to **Common Stock Analysis** and press the ⟨**Enter**⟩ key. The Common Stock Analysis Problems Menu appears. From this menu, the appropriate submodule can be accessed using a similar procedure.

Common Stock Analysis has been divided into three parts. The first part deals with the margin requirements for buying stock. Problems are presented for both the long and short position of common stock. The second part of the module deals with calculating stock returns, and the third part deals with calculating the value of the stock based on its future dividend stream. The valuation calculations use a simple constant growth model and a more complex multi-stage growth model.

NOTATION

The following is the list of symbols used in the formulae in this chapter:

m_i = Initial margin

m_a = Actual margin

m_m = Maintenance margin

MP = Market price of the stock

PP = Purchase price of the stock

SP = Sale price of the stock

D_0 = Current dividend on the stock

D_1 = The next expected dividend on the stock (in year 1)

D_t = The dividend in year t

k_e = Required rate of return on the stock

HPY = Holding period yield

ARR_a = Arithmetic average rate of return

ARR_g = Geometric average rate of return

P_0 = Current price of the stock

P_t = Price of the stock at time t

g_s = Supernormal growth rate in dividends

g = Normal growth rate in dividends

MARGIN—PURCHASES

This submodule calculates the actual margin based on the current market price of the common stock as well as the price of the stock at which the investor will receive a margin call from the stockbroker. This information will allow the investor to place a stop-loss order in to limit his losses. An investor will purchase stock on the margin only if there is an expectation that the price of the stock is going to rise. The price of the stock at a margin call will always be below the purchase price of the stock.

The submodule also presents the balance sheet of the margin account of the investor. A curious investor can use this submodule to perform sensitivity analysis on his margin account to determine his equity in the margin account at various stock prices.

The equation for calculating the actual margin percentage of a stock that was purchased on margin is:

$$m_a = \frac{MP - (1 - m_i) \times PP}{MP}$$

The equation for calculating the market price of a stock at a margin call is:

$$MP = \frac{(1 - m_i) \times PP}{(1 - m_m)}$$

The balance sheet amounts are calculated using the following simple rules:

Assets = Market Price of the Stock $\times$ # of Shares Purchased

Liabilities = Purchase Price of the Stock $\times$ # of Shares Purchased $\times$ (1 $-$ Initial Margin)

Equity = Assets $-$ Liabilities

To access this submodule, move the highlight bar to **Margin $-$ Purchase**. Press the ⟨**Enter**⟩ key and the data entry screen will appear.

Sample Problem

Helena Company's stock is currently selling for $15 per share. The initial margin requirement is 55 percent and the maintenance margin requirement is 35 percent. Cap Anson buys 100 shares of Helena stock on margin. To what price must the stock fall for Cap to receive a margin call?*

*Problem from *Investments* by William F. Sharpe and Gordon J. Alexander. © 1990 by Prentice Hall, Inc. Reprinted with permission from Prentice Hall, Inc.

This problem can be solved for the market price at which a margin call is received from the broker as follows:

$$MP = [(1 - 0.55) \times 15]/(1 - 0.35) = \$10.38$$

The software solution for this problem can be obtained by entering the following data:

Purchase Price   = 15

Market Price   = 25   (Any number will do!)

Initial Margin   = 55

Maintenance Margin   = 35

Number of Shares   = 100

When the variables are entered on the **Stock Data for Margin Analysis** screen, it will appear as in Figure 4.1. After making sure that all data are entered correctly, highlight **Show Results** on the menu bar and press the ⟨**Enter**⟩ key. The **Analysis of Margin Purchase** screen will appear, which is shown in Figure 4.2.

Move the highlight bar to **New Input** and press ⟨**Enter**⟩ to continue with the next problem.

Sample Problem

Assume an investor buys 100 shares of stock at $50 per share, putting up a 70 percent margin. Maintenance margin is 30 percent. If the stock rises to $80 per share, what would be the investor's new margin position?*

This problem requires that the investor's actual margin should be calculated as follows:

$$\text{Actual margin} = (80 - (1 - 0.70) \times 50)/80$$
$$= 65/80 = .8125 = 81.25\%$$

Fig. 4.1

```
        Stock Data for Margin Analysis

        Purchase Price($):     15.000

          Market Price($):     25.000

        Initial Margin(%):     55.00

    Maintenance Margin(%):     35.00

        Number of Shares:       100
```

Please hit the <ENTER> key after entering data in each field

```
Edit Input                                    Show Results
```

*Problem from *Fundamentals of Investments* by Lawrence J. Gitman and Michael D. Joehnk. © 1990 by Lawrence J. Gitman and Michael D. Joehnk. Reprinted with Permission from HarperCollins Publishers.

Fig. 4.2

```
┌─────────────────────────────────────────────────────────┐
│                Analysis of Margin Purchase               │
│        Actual Margin (%)=         73.00                   │
│        Stock Price at Margin Call ($)=     10.38          │
│             Balance Sheet of Margin Account              │
│        Assets       2500.00   Liabilities      675.00    │
│                               Equity          1825.00    │
└─────────────────────────────────────────────────────────┘
```

```
┌──────────────────┐
│  Print Results   │     Edit Input       New Input      Stock Menu
└──────────────────┘
```

The software solution of this problem would require the entry of the following data:

Purchase Price   = 50
Market Price   = 80
Initial Margin   = 70
Maintenance Margin   = 30
Number of Shares   = 100

When the variables are entered on the **Stock Data for Margin Analysis** screen, it will appear as in Figure 4.3. After making sure that all data are entered correctly, highlight **Show Results** on the menu bar and press the ⟨**Enter**⟩ key. The Analysis of Margin Purchase screen will appear, which is shown in Figure 4.4.

Move the highlight bar to **New Input** and press ⟨**Enter**⟩ to continue with the next problem.

Fig. 4.3

```
┌─────────────────────────────────────────────────────┐
│           Stock Data for Margin Analysis            │
│           Purchase Price($):    50.000              │
│             Market Price($):    80.000              │
│            Initial Margin(%):   70.00               │
│       Maintenance Margin(%):    30.00               │
│           Number of Shares:     100                 │
└─────────────────────────────────────────────────────┘
```

```
Please hit the <ENTER> key after entering data in each field
┌──────────────────┐
│   Edit Input     │                      Show Results
└──────────────────┘
```

Fig. 4.4

```
┌─────────────────────────────────────────────────────────────┐
│                                                               │
│              Analysis of Margin Purchase                      │
│      Actual Margin (%)=          81.25                        │
│      Stock Price at Margin Call ($)=     21.43                │
│               Balance Sheet of Margin Account                 │
│      Assets      8000.00    Liabilities      1500.00          │
│                             Equity           6500.00          │
│                                                               │
└─────────────────────────────────────────────────────────────┘
```

```
┌─────────────────┐
│  Print Results  │          Edit Input        New Input      Stock Menu
└─────────────────┘
```

Sample Problem

Consider the following information:

Stock price per share	$60
Margin requirement	50%
Interest rate on margin acct.	9%
Maintenance margin	30%

Ignoring transaction costs and taxes, assume that an investor takes a long position using margin. Calculate the stock price that will trigger a margin call.*

The market price at which a margin call will be triggered is calculated using the above formula as follows:*

$$MP = [(1 - 0.50) \times 60]/(1 - 0.30)$$
$$= 30/0.70 = 0.4286 = \$42.86$$

Enter the following data to get the software solution of the problem:

Purchase Price	= 60	
Market Price	= 50	(Any price would do!)
Initial Margin	= 50	
Maintenance Margin	= 30	
Number of Shares	= 100	(Any number would do!)

When the variables are entered on the Stock Data for Margin Analysis screen, it will appear as in Figure 4.5. After making sure that all data are entered correctly, highlight **Show Results** on the menu bar and press the ⟨**Enter**⟩ key. The Analysis of Margin Purchase screen will appear, which is shown in Figure 4.6.

---

*Problem from *Investments: Analysis, Selection and Management* by Edward A. Moses and John M. Cheney. © 1989 by West Publishing Company. Reprinted with permission from West Publishing Company.

Fig. 4.5

```
┌─────────────────────────────────────────────────┐
│                                                   │
│          Stock Data for Margin Analysis           │
│                                                   │
│            Purchase Price($):    60.000           │
│                                                   │
│              Market Price($):    50.000           │
│                                                   │
│             Initial Margin(%):    50.00           │
│                                                   │
│         Maintenance Margin(%):    30.00           │
│                                                   │
│              Number of Shares:      100           │
│                                                   │
└─────────────────────────────────────────────────┘
```

Please hit the <ENTER> key after entering data in each field

```
┌──────────────┐
│  Edit Input  │                      Show Results
└──────────────┘
```

This is the last problem in this area. Return to the Common Stock Analysis menu by moving the highlight bar to **Stock Menu** and pressing the ⟨**Enter**⟩ key.

MARGIN—SHORT SALES

This module calculates the current margin for a stock as well as the price of the stock at the margin call. An investor will sell a stock short only if there is an expectation that the price of the stock is going to decline. The current margin will become worse if the price of the stock goes up. The price of the stock at a margin call is always above the short sale price of the stock. The balance sheet of the margin account is also calculated.

The equation for calculating the actual margin for a short sale is:

$$m_a = \frac{SP \times (1 + m_i) - MP}{MP}$$

Fig. 4.6

```
┌─────────────────────────────────────────────────────┐
│                                                       │
│            Analysis of Margin Purchase                │
│                                                       │
│      Actual Margin (%)=         40.00                 │
│                                                       │
│      Stock Price at Margin Call ($)=    42.86         │
│                                                       │
│            Balance Sheet of Margin Account            │
│                                                       │
│      Assets      5000.00    Liabilities    3500.00    │
│                                                       │
│                             Equity         2000.00    │
│                                                       │
└─────────────────────────────────────────────────────┘
```

```
┌────────────────┐
│ Print Results  │      Edit Input        New Input      Stock Menu
└────────────────┘
```

The equation for calculating the market price of the common stock which will trigger a margin call is:

$$MP = \frac{SP \times (1 + m_i)}{1 + m_m}$$

This submodule can be accessed by moving the highlight bar to **Margin – Short Sales** and pressing the ⟨**Enter**⟩ key. The **Stock Data for Margin Analysis** screen will appear.

Sample Problem

Through a margin account, Candy Cummings sells short 200 shares of Madison Inc. stock for $50 per share. The initial margin requirement is 45 percent.

If Madison stock subsequently rises to $60 per share, what is the actual margin in Candy's account?*

$$\text{Actual Margin} = [50 \times (1 + 0.45) - 60]/60$$
$$= .2083 = 20.83\%$$

Enter the following data in the data entry screen to obtain the solution to this problem:

Short Sale Price	= 50	
Market Price	= 75	
Initial Margin	= 45	
Maintenance Margin	= 20	(Not provided, any number would do!)
Number of shares	= 200	

Enter these stock variables and the Stock Data for Margin Analysis screen will appear as shown in Figure 4.7. Highlight the choice **Show Results** and press

Fig. 4.7

```
┌─────────────────────────────────────────────────────┐
│                                                       │
│           Stock Data for Margin Analysis              │
│                                                       │
│        Short Sale Price($):   50.000                  │
│                                                       │
│            Market Price($):   75.000                  │
│                                                       │
│          Initial Margin(%):   45.00                   │
│                                                       │
│      Maintenance Margin(%):   20.00                   │
│                                                       │
│          Number of Shares:    200                     │
│                                                       │
└─────────────────────────────────────────────────────┘
```

Please hit the <ENTER> key after entering data in each field

```
┌─────────────────┐
│   Edit Input    │                           Show Results
└─────────────────┘
```

*Problem from *Investments* by William F. Sharpe and Gordon J. Alexander. © 1990 by Prentice Hall, Inc. Reprinted with permission from Prentice Hall, Inc.

Fig. 4.8

```
Analysis óf Short Sales on Margin

Actual Margin (%):    20.83

Stock Price at Margin Call ($):   60.42

Balance Sheet of Margin Account

Assets   14500.00      Liabilities    12000.00

                       Equity          2500.00
```

Print Results	Edit Input	New Input	Stock Menu

the ⟨**Enter**⟩ key and the Analysis of Short Sales on Margin screen will appear, which is shown in Figure 4.8.

Move the highlight bar to **New Input** and press the ⟨**Enter**⟩ key to continue working margin—short sale problems.

Sample Problem

Assume an investor short sells 100 shares of stock at $50 per share, putting up a 70 percent margin. Assume a maintenance margin of 30 percent. What is the new margin for this transaction if the price of the stock falls to $20 per share?*

The new margin or the actual margin for the account can be calculated as:

$$\text{Actual Margin} = [50 \times (1 + 0.70) - 20]/20$$
$$= 65/20 = 3.25 = 325\%$$

The following data need to be entered to find the solution to this problem using the software:

Short Sale Price	= 50
Market Price	= 20
Initial Margin	= 70
Maintenance Margin	= 30
Number of Shares	= 100

Enter these data in the Stock Data for Margin Analysis screen. The figures should appear as in Figure 4.9. Highlight **Show Results** on the menu bar. Press the ⟨**Enter**⟩ key and the Analysis of Short Sales on Margin screen will appear, which is shown in Figure 4.10.

Move the highlight bar to **New Input** and press ⟨**Enter**⟩ to continue working the problems.

*Problem from *Fundamentals of Investments* by Lawrence J. Gitman and Michael D. Joehnk. © 1990 by Lawrence J. Gitman and Michael D. Joehnk. Reprinted with Permission from HarperCollins Publishers.

Fig. 4.9

```
┌─────────────────────────────────────────────────┐
│                                                   │
│          Stock Data for Margin Analysis           │
│                                                   │
│          Short Sale Price($):   50.000            │
│                                                   │
│             Market Price($):   20.000             │
│                                                   │
│            Initial Margin(%):   70.00             │
│                                                   │
│        Maintenance Margin(%):   30.00             │
│                                                   │
│            Number of Shares:     100              │
│                                                   │
└─────────────────────────────────────────────────┘
```

Please hit the <ENTER> key after entering data in each field

┌──────────────┐
│ Edit Input │   Show Results
└──────────────┘

Sample Problem

Consider the following information:

Stock price per share $25
Margin requirement   50%
Maintenance margin   30%

Assume that an investor takes a short position with an equity deposit equal to 50 percent of the initial margin. Calculate the stock price that will trigger a margin call.*

Fig. 4.10

```
┌─────────────────────────────────────────────────┐
│                                                   │
│          Analysis of Short Sales on Margin        │
│                                                   │
│       Actual Margin (%):  325.00                  │
│                                                   │
│     Stock Price at Margin Call ($):   65.38       │
│                                                   │
│          Balance Sheet of Margin Account          │
│                                                   │
│     Assets    8500.00     Liabilities    2000.00  │
│                                                   │
│                            Equity        6500.00  │
│                                                   │
└─────────────────────────────────────────────────┘
```

┌──────────────────┐
│ Print Results   │   Edit Input   New Input   Stock Menu
└──────────────────┘

*Problem from *Investments: Analysis, Selection and Management* by Edward A. Moses and John M. Cheney. © 1989 by West Publishing Company. Reprinted with permission from West Publishing Company.

The market price that triggers a margin call in a short position can be calculated as follows:

$$MP = [25 \times (1 + 0.50)]/(1 + 0.30)$$
$$= \$28.85$$

The software solution needs the following input data:

Short Sale Price = 25

Market Price = 30   (Any positive number would do!)

Initial Margin = 50

Maintenance Margin = 30

Number of Shares = 100   (Guess!)

Enter these data in the Stock Data for Margin Analysis screen. The figures should appear as in Figure 4.11. Highlight the choice **Show Results** and press the ⟨**Enter**⟩ key. The Analysis of Short Sales on Margin screen will appear. This screen is shown in Figure 4.12.

This concludes the sample problems in this submodule. Move the highlight bar to **Stock Menu** and press ⟨**Enter**⟩. The next module may now be selected. Move the highlight bar to **Holding Period Yield** and press the ⟨**Enter**⟩ key. The Holding Period Yield Calculation screen will appear.

HOLDING PERIOD YIELD

This submodule calculates the total yield from holding a security over a period of time. The yield includes not only capital appreciation/depreciation but also cash flows such as dividends received by the investor during the period. It should be noted that the holding period yield is not necessarily an annualized yield because the period over which the yield is calculated may vary from one situation to another. The submodule also determines the holding period yield

Fig. 4.11

```
               Stock Data for Margin Analysis

           Short Sale Price($):    25.000

             Market Price($):      30.000

            Initial Margin(%):     50.00

       Maintenance Margin(%):      30.00

           Number of Shares:        100
```

Please hit the <ENTER> key after entering data in each field

```
Edit Input
```
                                        Show Results

Fig. 4.12

```
┌─────────────────────────────────────────────────────────┐
│                                                         │
│            Analysis of Short Sales on Margin            │
│         Actual Margin (%):    25.00                     │
│       Stock Price at Margin Call ($):   28.85           │
│            Balance Sheet of Margin Account              │
│      Assets    3750.00     Liabilities    3000.00       │
│                            Equity          750.00       │
│                                                         │
└─────────────────────────────────────────────────────────┘
```

Print Results	Edit Input	New Input	Stock Menu

for stocks purchased on margin. Purchasing stocks on margin is one way of increasing the financial leverage of the investor. The holding period yield will always be magnified by the use of margin. This, however, works both ways. If an investor loses money on a stock purchase, the use of margin will magnify the percentage loss.

The equation for the holding period yield is:

$$HPY = \frac{P_{End} - P_{beg} + CF}{P_{beg} \times (1 - m_i)}$$

In solving problems which do not involve a margin purchase, the initial margin percentage should be entered as "0."

To access the **Holding Period Yield** submodule, highlight the choice in the **Common Stock Analysis** and press the ⟨**Enter**⟩ key. The data entry screen for the submodule will appear.

Sample Problem

A fundamental analysis of DSK, Inc. resulted in the following:

Current stock price	$18.00
Estimate of stock's price in one year	$20.00
Estimate of dividends for next year	$2.50
Present yield on one-year Treasury bill	8.62%
Beta	1.50

Calculate the stock's expected one-year HPR.* The holding period yield for DSK stock will be calculated as follows:

$$HPR = (20 - 18 + 2.50)/18$$
$$= .25 \text{ or } 25\%$$

*Problem from *Investments: Analysis, Selection and Management* by Edward A. Moses and John M. Cheney. © 1989 by West Publishing Company. Reprinted with permission from West Publishing Company.

Fig. 4.13

```
┌──────────────────────────────────────────────────────────────┐
│                 Holding Period Yield Calculation              │
│                  Purchase Price of the Stock ($):   18.000     │
│     End-of-Period Market Price of the Stock ($):   20.000     │
│                  Cash Flow During the Period ($):    2.50      │
│                   Initial Margin Percentage (%):    0.00       │
│                                                                │
└──────────────────────────────────────────────────────────────┘
```

Please hit the <ENTER> key after entering data in each field

┌─────────────────┐
│   Edit Input   │   Show Results
└─────────────────┘

To solve this problem using the software, enter the following data:

Purchase Price of the Stock	= 18
End-of-Period Market Price of the Stock	= 20
Cash Flow During the Period	= 2.50
Initial Margin Percentage	= 0

On data entry, the Holding Period Yield Calculation screen will appear as in Figure 4.13. Highlight **Show Results** and press the ⟨**Enter**⟩ key and the Holding Period Yield Results screen will appear as seen in Figure 4.14.

Move the highlight bar to **New Input** and press the ⟨**Enter**⟩ key to continue working the problems.

Sample Problem

Tasty Foods, Inc., stock is currently selling for $35 per share. The stock is expected to pay a $1 dividend at the end of the next year. It is reliably

Fig. 4.14

```
┌──────────────────────────────────────────────────────────────┐
│                 Holding Period Yield Results                  │
│   1.   Capital Gains ($)=                          2.00       │
│                                                                │
│   2.   Cashflow in the Period ($)=                 2.50       │
│                                                                │
│   3.   Total Gains = (1) + (2) =                   4.50       │
│                                                                │
│   4.   Holding Period Yield without Margin (%)=   25.00       │
│                                                                │
│   5.   Holding Period Yield with Margin (%)=      25.00       │
└──────────────────────────────────────────────────────────────┘
```

┌─────────────────┐
│ Print Results │   Edit Input   New Input   Stock Menu
└─────────────────┘

estimated that the stock will sell for $37 at the end of one year. Assuming that the dividend and price forecasts are accurate, would you pay $35 today for the stock to hold it for one year if your required rate of return were 12 percent?*

$$\text{The } HPY \text{ for Tasty Foods} = (37 - 35 + 1)/35$$
$$= .0857 \text{ or } 8.57\%$$

Since the required rate of return on the stock, 12 percent, is greater than the expected rate of return, the stock is overpriced. In other words you would not pay $35 for the stock.

The software solution to this problem is obtained by entering the following data:

Purchase Price of the Stock	= 35
End-of-Period Market Price of the Stock	= 37
Cash Flow During the Period	= 1
Initial Margin Percentage	= 0

The Holding Period Yield Calculation screen will appear as in Figure 4.15. Highlight **Show Results** and press the ⟨**Enter**⟩ key and the Holding Period Yield Results screen will appear. This screen is shown in Figure 4.16.

Move the highlight bar to **New Input** and press the ⟨**Enter**⟩ key to continue working problems.

Sample Problem

Calculate the holding period return (*HPR*) for the following two investment alternatives.*

	Investment Vehicle	
	X	*Y*
Cash received		
1st quarter	$ 1.00	$ 0
2nd quarter	1.20	0
3rd quarter	0	0
4th quarter	2.30	2.00
Investment value		
End-of-year	29.00	56.00
Beginning-of-year	30.00	50.00

$$HPY_x = (29 - 30 + 1 + 1.2 + 0 + 2.3)/30$$
$$= .1167 \text{ or } 11.67\%$$
$$HPY_y = (56 - 50 + 2)/50$$
$$= .16 \text{ or } 16\%$$

*Problem from *Security Analysis and Portfolio Management* by Donald E. Fischer and Ronald J. Jordan. © 1991 by Prentice Hall, Inc. Reprinted with permission from Prentice Hall, Inc.

*Problem from *Fundamentals of Investments* by Lawrence J. Gitman and Michael D. Joehnk. © 1990 by Lawrence J. Gitman and Michael D. Joehnk. Reprinted with Permission from HarperCollins Publishers.

Fig. 4.15

```
┌──────────────────────────────────────────────────────────┐
│              Holding Period Yield Calculation            │
│                                                          │
│            Purchase Price of the Stock ($):   35.000     │
│                                                          │
│  End-of-Period Market Price of the Stock ($):   37.000   │
│                                                          │
│            Cash Flow During the Period ($):    1.00      │
│                                                          │
│              Initial Margin Percentage (%):    0.00      │
│                                                          │
└──────────────────────────────────────────────────────────┘
```

Please hit the <ENTER> key after entering data in each field

┌─────────────┐
│ Edit Input │   Show Results
└─────────────┘

The data for the software solution to the problem are:

	X	Y
Purchase Price	30	50
Market Price	29	56
Cash Flow	4.50	2
Initial Margin	0	0

Enter the data for investment X first. The screen would appear as in Figure 4.17. Highlight **Show Results** and press the ⟨**Enter**⟩ key and the Holding Period Yield Results screen will appear. This screen is shown in Figure 4.18.

Move the highlight bar to **New Input** and press ⟨**Enter**⟩ to enter data for investment Y. Once again, highlight the choice **Show Results** and press the ⟨**Enter**⟩ key and the Holding Period Results screen will appear. Compare the holding period yields for investment X and Y.

This concludes the discussion of sample problems in this submodule. Move the highlight bar to **Stock Menu** and press ⟨**Enter**⟩. The next module may

Fig. 4.16

```
┌──────────────────────────────────────────────────────────┐
│             Holding Period Yield Results                 │
│                                                          │
│   1.  Capital Gains ($)=                          2.00   │
│                                                          │
│   2.  Cashflow in the Period ($)=                 1.00   │
│                                                          │
│   3.  Total Gains = (1) + (2) =                   3.00   │
│                                                          │
│   4.  Holding Period Yield without Margin (%)=    8.57   │
│                                                          │
│   5.  Holding Period Yield with Margin (%)=       8.57   │
│                                                          │
└──────────────────────────────────────────────────────────┘
```

┌───────────────┐
│ Print Results │   Edit Input   New Input   Stock Menu
└───────────────┘

Fig. 4.17

```
┌─────────────────────────────────────────────────────────────┐
│              Holding Period Yield Calculation                 │
│                                                               │
│             Purchase Price of the Stock ($):   30.000         │
│                                                               │
│   End-of-Period Market Price of the Stock ($):  29.000        │
│                                                               │
│             Cash Flow During the Period ($):    4.50          │
│                                                               │
│             Initial Margin Percentage (%):      0.00          │
│                                                               │
└─────────────────────────────────────────────────────────────┘
```

Please hit the <ENTER> key after entering data in each field

┌──────────────┐
│ Edit Input   │   Show Results
└──────────────┘

now be selected. Move the highlight bar to **Average Rate of Return** and press the ⟨**Enter**⟩ key. The Average Rate of Return Calculation screen will appear.

AVERAGE RATE OF RETURN

On occasion, an investor may hold a security for several months (or years) before selling it for a profit. To gauge the performance of this investment, you should be able to estimate the average rate of return from the investment per month (or per year). This submodule will perform this analysis for the investor and present both the arithmetic and the geometric average rate of return.

The average rate of return is estimated from the holding period yield, *HPY*, as follows:

$$ARR_a = HPY/n$$
$$ARR_g = (1 + HPY)^{(1/n)} - 1$$

Fig. 4.18

```
┌─────────────────────────────────────────────────────────────┐
│              Holding Period Yield Results                     │
│                                                               │
│   1.  Capital Gains ($)=                          -1.00       │
│                                                               │
│   2.  Cashflow in the Period ($)=                  4.50       │
│                                                               │
│   3.  Total Gains = (1) + (2) =                    3.50       │
│                                                               │
│   4.  Holding Period Yield without Margin (%)=    11.67       │
│                                                               │
│   5.  Holding Period Yield with Margin (%)=       11.67       │
│                                                               │
└─────────────────────────────────────────────────────────────┘
```

┌──────────────────┐
│ Print Results   │   Edit Input   New Input   Stock Menu
└──────────────────┘

where n is the number of time periods (e.g., months or years) in the holding period.

Move the highlight bar to **Average Rate of Return** and press the ⟨**Enter**⟩ key to access this submodule. The data entry screen will appear.

Sample Problem

Jack Patton bought the stock of ABC Company at $25 and sold it six months later at $26.75. During these six months, he received cash dividends totaling $1.70 from the company. Calculate Jack's average monthly rate of return.

$$HPY = (26.75 - 25.00 + 1.70)/25.00$$
$$= .138 \text{ or } 13.8\%$$
$$ARR_a = .138/6 = .023 \text{ or } 2.3\%$$
$$ARR_g = (1.138)^{(1/6)} - 1 = .0218 \text{ or } 2.18\%$$

Enter the following information in the data entry screen to obtain the solution of this problem:

Beginning Price of the Stock ($)	= 25.00
Ending Price of the Stock ($)	= 26.75
Cash Flow During the Holding Period	= 1.70
Number of Time Periods in the Holding Period	= 6

The screen should appear as in Figure 4.19 after data entry. Highlight the choice **Show Results** and press the ⟨Enter⟩ key and the solution screen will appear as shown in Figure 4.20.

Move the highlight bar to **Stock Menu** and press the ⟨Enter⟩ key to get back to the menu for the submodule. Highlight the choice **Stock Price – Constant Growth** and press the ⟨Enter⟩ key to select the next submodule.

Fig. 4.19

```
┌────────────────────────────────────────────────────────┐
│          Average Rate of Return Calculation            │
│                                                        │
│         Beginning Price of The Stock ($):  25.000      │
│                                                        │
│           Ending Price of the Stock ($):  26.750      │
│                                                        │
│   Cash Flow During the Holding Period ($):   1.70     │
│                                                        │
│  Number of Time Periods in the Holding Period:    6   │
└────────────────────────────────────────────────────────┘
```

Please hit the <ENTER> key after entering data in each field

```
┌──────────────┐
│  Edit Input  │                        Show Results
└──────────────┘
```

Fig. 4.20

```
┌─────────────────────────────────────────────────────────────┐
│              Average Rate of Return Results                  │
│                                                              │
│   1. Capital Gains ($)=                              1.75    │
│                                                              │
│   2. Cash Flow in the Period ($)=                    1.70    │
│                                                              │
│   3. Total Gains = (1) + (2) =                       3.45    │
│                                                              │
│   4. Holding Period Return (%)=                     13.80    │
│                                                              │
│   5. Arithmetic Average Rate of Return (%)=          2.30    │
│                                                              │
│   6. Geometric Average Rate of Return (%)=           2.18    │
└─────────────────────────────────────────────────────────────┘
```

```
┌─────────────────┐
│  Print Results  │       Edit Input        New Input        FM Menu
└─────────────────┘
```

CONSTANT GROWTH STOCK PRICE

The fundamental principle in valuation of a financial asset is that the market value of a financial asset is the **capitalization of income** method of valuation. This method determines the value of a financial asset as the sum of the present values of all future cash flows derived from the asset. This is expressed in the following equation:

$$V = \sum_{t=1}^{\infty} \frac{CF_t}{(1 + k)^t}$$

where k is the discount rate commensurate with risk of the cash flow stream and CF_t is the cash flow at time t. This principle, however, is difficult to apply in real world applications such as the valuation of common stock which is expected yield cash flow for an indefinite period of time. The only way to put the principle in practice is to make simplifying assumptions about the nature of the infinite cash flow stream. If you assume that the amount of cash flow is growing at a constant rate of growth from year to year, then it is easy to derive the following model, which is known as the Gordon Growth Model:

$$P_0 = \frac{D_1}{k_e - g}$$

Move the highlight bar to **Price − Constant Growth** and press the ⟨**Enter**⟩ key to access this submodule. The **Stock Data for Price Calculation** screen will appear.

While entering data for problems in this segment, it should be remembered that the numerator in the above formula is the cash dividend to be paid in year 1. Some problems do not provide this information, but specify the current dividend, which is the cash dividend received in year 0. The data input screen is designed to accept either kind of information.

Sample Problem

The Bourke Basketball Company (BBC) earned $5 a share last year and paid a dividend of $3 a share. Next year, you expect the company to earn $5.50 and continue its payout ratio. Assuming you expect a 5 percent dividend yield a year from now when you anticipate selling the stock, how much would you be willing to pay for it?*

The price of BBC can be found by applying the constant growth model described above as follows:

$$D_1 = \$5.50 \times 3/5 = \$3.30$$
$$P_0 = \$3.30/.05 \quad \text{(Recall that the denominator in the}$$
$$\text{Gordon Model is the Dividend Yield)}$$
$$= \$66.00$$

It should be noted that the dividend yield of 5 percent is the same as the denominator in the previous equation.

Since the problem provides the necessary information in a roundabout manner, data for the growth rate and the required rate of return must be calculated first.

$$\text{Expected Growth Rate} = 5.50/5.00 - 1 = .10 \text{ or } 10\%$$
$$\text{Required Rate of Return} = 10 + 5 = 15\%$$

Enter the following information in the data entry screen to obtain the solution to this problem:

Dividend Amount	= 3.30
Year in Which Dividend Received	= 1 (Next year's dividend)
Growth Rate in Dividends	= 10
Required Rate of Return	= 15

The screen should appear as in Figure 4.21 after data entry. Highlight the choice **Show Results** and press the ⟨**Enter**⟩ key and the **Stock Price — Constant Growth Stock** screen will appear, which is shown in Figure 4.22.

Move the highlight bar to **New Input** and press the ⟨**Enter**⟩ key to input data for the next sample problem in the submodule.

Sample Problem

Lenn Industries just paid a cash dividend on its stock of $2 per share. The earnings and dividends of the company are expected to grow at an annual rate

---

*Problem from *Investments* by Frank K. Reilly. © 1986 by CBS College Publishing. Reprinted with permission from The Dryden Press.

Fig. 4.21

```
┌─────────────────────────────────────────────────────────────┐
│                                                              │
│              Stock Data for Price Calculation                │
│                    Dividend Amount ($):      3.30            │
│     Year in which Dividend Received (0 or 1):       1        │
│          Growth Rate in Dividends (%):      10.00            │
│          Required Rate of Return (%):      15.00            │
│                                                              │
└─────────────────────────────────────────────────────────────┘
```

        Please hit <ENTER> key after entering data in each field

    ┌─────────────┐
    │ Edit Input │   Show Results
    └─────────────┘

of 12 percent indefinitely. Investors expect a rate of return on Lenn's shares of 14 percent. What is a fair price for this company's shares?*

The solution to the problem is:

$$D_1 = 2.00 \times 1.12 = \$2.24 \quad \text{(Next year's dividend)}$$
$$\text{Stock Price} = 2.24/(.14 - .12)$$
$$= \$112.00$$

Enter the following data to find the solution using the software:

Dividend Amount   = 2.00

Year in Which Dividend Received   = 0   (Current Dividend)

Growth Rate in Dividends   = 12

Required Rate of Return   = 14

The screen should appear as in Figure 4.23. Highlight **Show Results** and press the ⟨**Enter**⟩ key to bring up the solution of the problem. This screen is shown in Figure 4.24.

Fig. 4.22

```
┌─────────────────────────────────────────────────────────────┐
│                                                              │
│           Stock Price - Constant Growth Stock                │
│                                                              │
│     Cash Dividend in Year 1 ($) =       3.30                │
│                                                              │
│     Dividend Yield = Required ROR - Growth Rate =  0.050    │
│                                                              │
│     Stock Price ($) = Cash Div. ÷ Div. Yld. =   66.00      │
│                                                              │
└─────────────────────────────────────────────────────────────┘
```

    ┌─────────────────┐
    │ Print Results   │   Edit Input   New Input   Stock Menu
    └─────────────────┘

        *Problem from *Security Analysis and Portfolio Management* by Donald E. Fischer and Ronald J. Jordan. © 1991 by Prentice Hall, Inc. Reprinted with permission from Prentice Hall, Inc.

Fig. 4.23

```
┌─────────────────────────────────────────────────────────────┐
│                                                               │
│              Stock Data for Price Calculation                 │
│                                                               │
│                  Dividend Amount ($):     2.00                │
│                                                               │
│   Year in which Dividend Received (0 or 1):      0            │
│                                                               │
│        Growth Rate in Dividends (%):     12.00                │
│                                                               │
│        Required Rate of Return (%):      14.00                │
│                                                               │
│                                                               │
└─────────────────────────────────────────────────────────────┘
```

Please hit <ENTER> key after entering data in each field

| Edit Input | Show Results

Move the highlight bar to **New Input** and press ⟨**Enter**⟩ to continue working problems.

Sample Problem

Jackson Information Services currently pays a dividend of $5.00 per share on its common stock. The dividend is expected to grow at 4 percent per year forever. Stocks with similar risk currently are priced to provide a 12 percent expected return. What is the intrinsic value of Jackson stock?*

The problem can be solved as follows:

$$D_1 = \$5.00 \times 1.04 = \$5.20$$
$$\text{Stock Price} = 5.20/(.12 - .04)$$
$$= \$65.00$$

To obtain the software solution to the problem, enter the following data:

Dividend Amount   = 5

Year in Which Dividend Received   = 0

Fig. 4.24

```
┌─────────────────────────────────────────────────────────────┐
│                                                               │
│           Stock Price - Constant Growth Stock                 │
│                                                               │
│    Cash Dividend in Year 1 ($) =       2.24                   │
│                                                               │
│    Dividend Yield = Required ROR - Growth Rate =   0.020      │
│                                                               │
│    Stock Price ($) = Cash Div. ÷ Div. Yld. =   112.00         │
│                                                               │
└─────────────────────────────────────────────────────────────┘
```

| Print Results | Edit Input   New Input   Stock Menu

*Problem from *Investments* by William F. Sharpe and Gordon J. Alexander. © 1990 by Prentice Hall, Inc. Reprinted with permission from Prentice Hall, Inc.

Fig. 4.25

```
┌─────────────────────────────────────────────────────────────┐
│              Stock Data for Price Calculation                │
│                                                               │
│                    Dividend Amount ($):    5.00              │
│                                                               │
│     Year in which Dividend Received (0 or 1):       0        │
│                                                               │
│             Growth Rate in Dividends (%):   4.00             │
│                                                               │
│             Required Rate of Return (%):   12.00             │
│                                                               │
└─────────────────────────────────────────────────────────────┘
```

        Please hit <ENTER> key after entering data in each field

┌──────────────┐
│ Edit Input │   Show Results
└──────────────┘

Growth Rate in Dividends   = 4
Required Rate of Return   = 12

Enter these data in the **Stock Data for Price Calculation** screen which should appear as in Figure 4.25. Highlight **Show Results** and press the ⟨**Enter**⟩ key and the **Stock Price − Constant Growth Stock** screen will appear as shown in Figure 4.26.

Move the highlight bar to **New Input** and press ⟨**Enter**⟩ to continue working problems.

Sample Problem

The FI Corporation's dividends per share are expected to grow indefinitely by 5 percent per year. If this year's year-end dividend is $8 and the market capitalization rate is 10 percent per year, what must the current stock price be?*

Fig. 4.26

```
┌─────────────────────────────────────────────────────────────┐
│              Stock Price - Constant Growth Stock             │
│                                                               │
│    Cash Dividend in Year 1 ($) =        5.20                 │
│                                                               │
│    Dividend Yield = Required ROR - Growth Rate =  0.080      │
│                                                               │
│    Stock Price ($) = Cash Div. ÷ Div. Yld. =    65.00        │
│                                                               │
└─────────────────────────────────────────────────────────────┘
```

┌────────────────┐
│ Print Results │   Edit Input   New Input   Stock Menu
└────────────────┘

*Problem from *Investments* by Zvi Bodie, Alex Kane and Alan J. Marcus. 1989 by Richard D. Irwin. Reprinted with permission from Richard D. Irwin.

Fig. 4.27

```
┌─────────────────────────────────────────────────────────┐
│                                                         │
│          Stock Data for Price Calculation               │
│                                                         │
│                    Dividend Amount ($):    8.00         │
│                                                         │
│   Year in which Dividend Received (0 or 1):    0        │
│                                                         │
│         Growth Rate in Dividends (%):    5.00           │
│                                                         │
│        Required Rate of Return (%):   10.00             │
│                                                         │
└─────────────────────────────────────────────────────────┘
```

Please hit <ENTER> key after entering data in each field

```
┌──────────────┐
│  Edit Input  │                                Show Results
└──────────────┘
```

This problem uses different terms to provide the data needed to find the stock price.

$$D_1 = \$8.00 \times 1.05 = \$8.40$$
$$\text{Stock Price} = 8.40/(.10 - .05)$$
$$= \$168.00$$

The following data need to be entered to find the solution to this problem using the software:

Dividend Amount   = 8
Year in Which Dividend Received = 0
Growth Rate in Dividends   = 5
Required Rate of Return   = 10

After data entry, **Stock Data for Price Calculation** screen will appear as in Figure 4.27. Highlight the choice **Show Results** and press the ⟨**Enter**⟩ key and the **Stock Price − Constant Growth Stock** screen will appear. This screen is shown in Figure 4.28.

Fig. 4.28

```
┌─────────────────────────────────────────────────────────┐
│                                                         │
│           Stock Price - Constant Growth Stock           │
│                                                         │
│     Cash Dividend in Year 1 ($) =      8.40             │
│                                                         │
│   Dividend Yield = Required ROR - Growth Rate =  0.050  │
│                                                         │
│   Stock Price ($) = Cash Div. ÷ Div. Yld. =  168.00     │
│                                                         │
└─────────────────────────────────────────────────────────┘
```

```
┌────────────────┐
│ Print Results  │      Edit Input       New Input      Stock Menu
└────────────────┘
```

Sample Problem

The **Price—Constant Growth** module can also be used solve problems where stock dividends are expected to remain constant in perpetuity, because constant stock dividends imply a zero growth rate.

The BT&T Company's stock is expected to pay a cash dividend of $2.25 this year and in all future years. If the required rate of return on the stock is 13 percent, how much should the stock sell for in the market?

$$\text{The stock price} = \$2.25/0.13$$
$$= \$17.31$$

The data needed to solve the problem using the software are:

Dividend Amount   = 2.25

Year in Which Dividend Received   = 0

Growth Rate in Dividends   = 0

Required Rate of Return   = 13

Enter the above data in the **Stock Data for Price Calculation** screen which will appear as in Figure 4.29. Highlight the choice **Show Results** and press the ⟨**Enter**⟩ key and the **Stock Price – Constant Growth Stock** screen will appear. This screen is shown in Figure 4.30.

This example concludes the discussion of the **Price – Constant Growth** submodule. To access the next submodule, return to the **Common Stock Analysis Menu**, highlight the choice **Price – Supernormal Growth** and press the ⟨**Enter**⟩ key. This will bring up the data entry screen for the next submodule.

Fig. 4.29

```
┌─────────────────────────────────────────────────────────┐
│              Stock Data for Price Calculation            │
│                    Dividend Amount ($):    2.25          │
│     Year in which Dividend Received (0 or 1):    0       │
│            Growth Rate in Dividends (%):    0.00         │
│            Required Rate of Return (%):    13.00         │
│                                                          │
└─────────────────────────────────────────────────────────┘
```

         Please hit <ENTER> key after entering data in each field

┌──────────────────┐
│   Edit Input   │   Show Results
└──────────────────┘

Fig. 4.30

```
┌─────────────────────────────────────────────────────────────┐
│                                                             │
│ │           Stock Price - Constant Growth Stock           │ │
│ │                                                         │ │
│ │  Cash Dividend in Year 1 ($) =        2.25              │ │
│ │                                                         │ │
│ │  Dividend Yield = Required ROR - Growth Rate =  0.130   │ │
│ │                                                         │ │
│ │  Stock Price ($) = Cash Div. ÷ Div. Yld. =    17.31     │ │
│ │                                                         │ │
│ └─────────────────────────────────────────────────────────┘ │
│                                                             │
└─────────────────────────────────────────────────────────────┘
```

┌─────────────────┐
│ Print Results   │   Edit Input   New Input   Stock Menu
└─────────────────┘

SUPERNORMAL GROWTH STOCK PRICE

A better method of determining the intrinsic value of a stock is to use the supernormal growth approach. This approach does away with the unrealistic assumption of a single constant growth rate applying to all future cash dividends to be received from a stock. A more realistic assumption is to assume that a firm's dividends and earnings are likely to grow rapidly over the first few years and then slow down. The slow-down phase is the phase in which dividends are assumed to grow at a constant growth rate for the foreseeable future. The **capitalization of income method of valuation** is then applied to the dividend stream to obtain the following equation:

$$P_0 = \sum_{t=1}^{T} \frac{D_0 (1 + g_s)^t}{(1 + k_e)^t} + \frac{D_0 (1 + g_s)^T (1 + g)}{k_e - g} \times \frac{1}{(1 + k_e)^T}$$

The term T in the above equation is the period of the so-called supernormal growth.

The submodule is accessed by moving the highlight bar to **Price—Supernormal Growth** and pressing the ⟨**Enter**⟩ key. The **Price Calculation for Supernormal Growth Stock** screen will appear.

Sample Problem

The Duo Growth Company just paid a dividend of $1 per share. The dividend is expected to grow at a rate of 25 percent per year for the next 3 years and then to level off to 5 percent per year forever. You think the appropriate market capitalization rate is 20 percent per year. What is your estimate of the intrinsic value of a share of the stock?*

To solve this problem without the help of the software, cash dividends for the first three years and the stock price at the end of year three need to be

---

*Problem from *Investments* by Zvi Bodie, Alex Kane and Alan J. Marcus. 1989 by Richard D. Irwin. Reprinted with permission from Richard D. Irwin.

calculated. These amounts will then be discounted back to their present value to determine the price of the stock.

$$D_1 = \$1.00 \times 1.25$$
$$= \$1.25$$
$$D_2 = \$1.25 \times 1.25$$
$$= \$1.56$$
$$D_3 = \$1.56 \times 1.25$$
$$= \$1.95$$

We would also need to calculate D_4 to determine the stock price, P_3.

$$D_4 = \$1.95 \times 1.05$$
$$= \$2.05$$
$$P_3 = D_4/(K_e - g)$$
$$= \$2.05/(.20 - .05)$$
$$= \$13.65$$

The stock price is the present value of the above four cash flows:

$$P_0 = \$1.25 \times 0.8333 + 1.56 \times 0.6944 + (1.95 + 13.65) \times 0.5787$$
$$= \$11.15$$

The following data are needed to obtain the software solution to this problem:

Number of Years of Supernormal Growth   = 3
Supernormal Growth Rate   = 25
Constant Growth Rate after Supernormal Growth   = 5
Current Dividend (in Year 0) Amount   = 1.00
Required Rate of Return on the Stock   = 20

The input screen is shown in Figure 4.31. After entering the above data in the input screen, highlight the choice **Show Results** in the menu bar and press

Fig. 4.31

```
┌─────────────────────────────────────────────────────────────────┐
│              Price Calculation for Supernormal Growth Stock        │
│                                                                    │
│               Number of Years of Supernormal Growth:        3      │
│                                                                    │
│                         Supernormal Growth Rate (%):     25.00     │
│                                                                    │
│  Constant Growth Rate after Supernormal Growth (%):       5.00     │
│                                                                    │
│            Current Dividend (in Year 0) Amount ($):       1.00     │
│                                                                    │
│            Required rate of Return on the Stock (%):     20.00     │
│                                                                    │
└─────────────────────────────────────────────────────────────────┘


        Please hit the <ENTER> key after entering data in each field
   ┌──────────────┐
   │  Edit Input  │                                    Show Results
   └──────────────┘
```

Fig. 4.32

```
┌─────────────────────────────────────────────────────────┐
│                                                         │
│         Stock Price - Supernormal Growth Stock          │
│                  Cash-Flow           Present Value      │
│       Year 1        1.25                 1.04           │
│       Year 2        1.56                 1.08           │
│       Year 3        1.95                 1.13           │
│       Year 3       13.65                 7.90           │
│                                                         │
│   Stock Price = Sum of the Present Values =   11.15     │
│                                                         │
└─────────────────────────────────────────────────────────┘
```

| Print Results | Edit Input | New Input | Stock Menu |

the ⟨**Enter**⟩ key. The **Stock Price − Supernormal Growth Stock** screen will appear. This screen is shown in Figure 4.32.

Move the highlight bar to **New Input** and press ⟨**Enter**⟩ to continue working problems.

Sample Problem

The Spirer Co. has common shares outstanding which had a dividend last year of $1.50. Investors have traditionally required a rate of return on these shares of 20 percent. Forecasts suggest that earnings and dividends will grow at a rate of 15 percent over the next five years and at a rate of 10 percent thereafter. What is the present value of the stock?*
The cash dividends for the first five years are:

Year	Cash Dividend ($)
1	1.73
2	1.98
3	2.28
4	2.62
5	3.02

and the stock price at the end of this period = $33.19
Discounting all these cash flows back to their present values and adding them up, the stock price is calculated as:

$$P_0 = \$19.95$$

The data to be entered in the input screen to obtain the software solution to this problem are:

Number of Years of Supernormal Growth   = 5

Supernormal Growth Rate   = 15

Constant Growth Rate after Supernormal Growth = 10

*Problem from *Security Analysis and Portfolio Management* by Donald E. Fischer and Ronald J. Jordan. © 1991 by Prentice Hall, Inc. Reprinted with permission from Prentice Hall, Inc.

Fig. 4.33

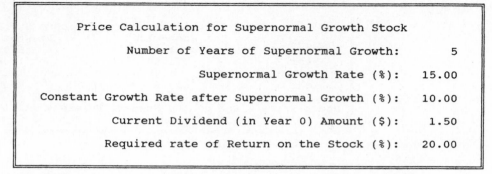

```
            Price Calculation for Supernormal Growth Stock
                    Number of Years of Supernormal Growth:       5
                               Supernormal Growth Rate (%):    15.00
        Constant Growth Rate after Supernormal Growth (%):    10.00
                    Current Dividend (in Year 0) Amount ($):    1.50
                    Required rate of Return on the Stock (%):   20.00
```

Please hit the <ENTER> key after entering data in each field

Edit Input   Show Results

Current Dividend (in Year 0) Amount ($)   = 1.50

Required Rate of Return on the Stock   = 20

Enter these data in the input screen. The screen should appear as shown in Figure 4.33. To bring up the solution, highlight the choice **Show Results** and press the ⟨**Enter**⟩ key. The solution is shown in Figure 4.34.

This concludes the discussion of the **Common Stock Analysis** module. To access any of the remaining modules, highlight the choice **Stock Menu** on the menu bar in the solution screen of the above problem and press the ⟨**Enter**⟩ key. This will bring up the **Common Stock Analysis** menu. Use the down arrow key to move the highlight bar to the choice **main menu** and press ⟨**Enter**⟩. This will pass the control to the main menu from which any other module can be selected.

Fig. 4.34

```
              Stock Price - Supernormal Growth Stock
                        Cash-Flow              Present Value
          Year 1          1.73                    1.44
          Year 2          1.98                    1.38
          Year 3          2.28                    1.32
          Year 4          2.62                    1.26
          Year 5          3.02                    1.21
          Year 5         33.92                   13.34

      Stock Price = Sum of the Present Values =  19.95
```

Print Results   Edit Input   New Input   Stock Menu

5 *Analysis of Hybrid Securities*

A modern day investor has many choices of investments other than stocks and bonds which offer attractive returns with limited risks. Call and put options, as well as convertible bonds are two such alternative investments. Since options and convertible bonds cannot be classified either as stocks or as bonds, they are usually classified as hybrid securities. This module in the **Investment Problem Solver** deals with the analysis of options and convertible bonds.

Analysis of call and put options is a relatively new topic in the theory of investments. Fischer Black and Myron Scholes developed the option pricing model in 1974. Since then, the securities industry has introduced options on stocks, treasury bonds, commodity futures, foreign currency futures, stock indexes, and stock index futures.

Convertible bonds offer an attractive investment instrument due to their convertibility feature. This feature allows an investor to exchange a bond for a predetermined number of shares of the issuing firm's common stock at a fixed price. Thus, an investor has the chance of participating in the firm's growth if the firm's investment plans bear fruit. Otherwise, the investor has the downside protection of owning a debt security issued by the firm on which a fixed amount of interest has to be paid annually. Because of its nature, a convertible bond can be thought of as a straight bond with a number of call options attached to it.

The **Analysis of Hybrid Securities** module contains the following submodules:

1. Option Pricing
2. Put-Call Parity—Put Price
3. Put-Call Parity—Call Price
4. Implied Volatility
5. Convertible Bond Analysis

The first submodule employs the Black-Scholes option pricing model to calculate the prices of a call and a put option. The submodule requires input of five variables affecting the option prices.

The next two submodules determine the price of a put or a call option based on the price of a call or a put option with the same exercise price and the same maturity.

The third module calculates, using a trial and error procedure, the volatility of the underlying security based on the call option price. The implied volatility is one variable which cannot be directly calculated without the availability of historical data on the underlying security. And again, volatility is subject to constant fluctuations due to changes in the perception of investors. This submodule can provide the up-to-date estimate of implied volatility for any security based on the most recent call option price and other variables which are available from the financial pages of any newspaper.

The last submodule accepts data related to the convertible bond characteristics and provides a detailed report about the bond's investment value (as a straight bond), the conversion parity price, and different types of premiums usually associated with a convertible bond.

GETTING STARTED

To access this module from the main menu, highlight **Analysis of Hybrid Securities** and press the ⟨**Enter**⟩ key. This will bring up the **Analysis of Hybrid Securities** menu. Move the highlight bar to the desired submodule and again press ⟨**Enter**⟩. This will bring up the data entry screen of the submodule of choice.

NOTATION

In the subsequent discussion, a number of symbols will be used. The following is a list of variables represented by the respective symbols:

P_c = Price of a call option

P_p = Price of a put option

R_f = Risk-free rate of return

E = Exercise or strike price of the option

S = Price of the underlying security

σ = Volatility of the underlying security

T = Term to expiry of the option, in years

$N(X)$ = Area under the normal distribution curve from minus infinity to X

V = Market price of the convertible bond

V_d = Straight bond value of the convertible bond (also known as the investment value of the bond)

V_c = Conversion value of the convertible bond

CR = Conversion ratio (number of shares/bond)

I = Coupon payment on the convertible bond

K = Yield-to-maturity on similar risk straight bonds

n = Term-to-maturity of the convertible bond

M = Face value of the convertible bond

CALL OPTION PRICING

A call option gives the buyer of the option a right (but with no obligation) to purchase one share of the underlying security at a fixed price within a specified period. A put option, on the other hand, gives the buyer of the option a right (but, again, with no obligation) to sell one share of the underlying security at a fixed price within a specified period.

Before investing in an option, the investor must determine the theoretical value of the option to decide if the option is correctly priced in the market. The Black-Scholes option pricing model is the most widely used model to calculate the price of a call option. The value of the option is a function of the stock price, the strike price, the risk-free rate, the time to expiration of the option, and the volatility of the underlying stock. The following set of equations is used to calculate the price of a call option:

$$P_c = SN(d_1) - Ee^{-R_f T}N(d_2)$$

where

$$d_1 = \frac{\ln\left(\frac{S}{E}\right) + \left(R_f + \frac{\sigma^2}{2}\right)T}{\sigma\sqrt{T}}$$

and

$$d_2 = d_1 - \sigma\sqrt{T}$$

You should keep in mind that the option pricing model applies only to those stocks which are expected to pay no cash dividends until the option expires.

The solution screen in this submodule presents both the call option price and the put option price for the same strike price and expiration date. In addition, the screen presents partial derivatives of the call option price with respect to the independent variables such as the stock price, days to expiration, strike price and the risk-free rate. The meaning and the application of these partial derivatives is as follows:

Delta $(\delta P_c/\delta S)$—Delta is the partial derivative of the call price with respect to the market price of the underlying stock. This factor represents the sensitivity of the call price to changes in the stock price when all other variables affecting the call option price are held constant. An investor can immunize his long position in a stock by selling delta number of calls. This is often referred to as **delta hedging**.

Theta ($\delta P_c/\delta\sigma$)—Theta of a call option is the rate of change of the call price with respect to time when all other variables affecting the call price remain unchanged. This factor will allow one to forecast the call price at a date in the immediate future if it can be assumed that all other variables will have the same value.

Lambda ($\delta P/\delta\sigma$)—This factor represents the sensitivity of the call option price to the change in the volatility of the returns from the asset underlying the call option. If the lambda factor of a call is high in absolute terms then the call price will be very sensitive to small changes in the volatility.

Gamma ($\delta\Delta/\delta S$)—his is the sensitivity of the delta factor of a call option price to the price of the underlying asset.

To access this submodule, move the highlight bar to **Call Option Pricing** and press the ⟨**Enter**⟩ key. At this point, the data entry screen will appear.

Sample Problem

Leonardo Equipment Co. stock currently sells at \$25. The company does not pay dividends. A six-month call option is available on the stock with an exercise price of \$25 and a premium of \$5. U.S. Treasury bills due in 182 days were just offered at auction at an annualized yield of 8 percent. The volatility of the stock over the past 26 weeks has been about 30 percent. Evaluate the option using the Black and Scholes Model.*

This problem can be solved as follows:

$$d_1 = (ln(25/25) + (.08 + 0.3 \times 0.3/2) \times 182/365) \div (0.3 \times \sqrt{(182/365)})$$
$$= 0.2942 \qquad \text{(Nearest number from the table)}$$
$$d_2 = 0.2942 - .2118412$$
$$= .0824$$
$$P_c = 25 \times .6147 - 25 \times .961 \times .5398$$
$$= \$2.40 \qquad \text{(Approximate price of the call)}$$

To find the price of the call option using the software, the following data need to be entered:

Stock Price	= 25
Strike Price	= 25
Risk-free Interest Rate	= 8
Time to Expiry in Days	= 182
Volatility (sigma) in decimals	= 0.30

Enter the above data in the data entry screen. The screen should appear as in Figure 5.1. Highlight the choice **Show Results** in the menu bar and press the ⟨**Enter**⟩ key and the Results of Option Calculation screen will appear. This screen is shown in Figure 5.2.

*Problem from *Security Analysis and Portfolio Management* by Donald E. Fischer and Ronald J. Jordan. © 1991 by Prentice Hall, Inc. Reprinted with permission from Prentice Hall, Inc.

Fig. 5.1

```
┌─────────────────────────────────────────────────────┐
│           Data For Option Price Calculation          │
│                 Stock Price ($):      25.000          │
│                Strike Price  ($):     25.000          │
│        Risk-free Interest Rate (%):    8.00           │
│              Time to Expiry in Days:    182           │
│        Volatility (Sigma) in decimals:  0.30          │
│                                                       │
└─────────────────────────────────────────────────────┘
```

Please hit the <ENTER> key after entering data in each field

| Edit Input | Show Results

To continue working problems, move the highlight bar to **New Input** and press ⟨**Enter**⟩.

Sample Problem

Consider the following data on a common stock and call option on the stock:

Stock price	= $50
Striking price	= $48
Time to expiry	= 3 months
Risk-free rate of return	= 8%
Variance of stock's return	= 0.25

Fig. 5.2

```
┌─────────────────────────────────────────────────────┐
│              Results of Option Calculations           │
│                 (Black-Scholes Model)                 │
│    Call Price ($):   2.59      Put Price ($):   1.62  │
│               Call Option Parameters                  │
│          Delta:   0.616        Theta:   -13.903       │
│          Lambda:  7.354        Gamma:    0.079        │
└─────────────────────────────────────────────────────┘
```

| Print Results | Edit Input   New Input   Hybrid Sec. Menu

Calculate the value of the option, using the Black-Scholes model.*

The solution to this problem is:

$$d_1 = (\ln(50/48) + (0.08 + 0.25/2) \times .25)/(\sqrt{0.25} \times \sqrt{0.25})$$
$$= 0.3683$$
$$d_2 = 0.3683 - \sqrt{0.25} \times \sqrt{0.25} = 0.1183$$

and

$$P_c = 50 \times 0.6443 - 48 \times 0.98 \times 0.5478$$
$$= \$6.45$$

To find the call option price using the software, the following input data are needed:

Stock Price	$= 50$
Strike Price	$= 48$
Risk-free Interest Rate	$= 8$
Time to Expiry in Days	$= 90$
Volatility (sigma) in decimals	$= 0.50$ ($\sqrt{0.25}$)

Enter the above data on the input screen. The screen is shown in Figure 5.3. Highlight the choice **Show Results** and press the ⟨**Enter**⟩ key and the Results of Option Calculations screen will appear, which is shown in Figure 5.4.

Move the highlight bar to **New Input** and press ⟨**Enter**⟩ to continue working problems.

Sample Problem

Use the Black-Scholes Option Pricing model to calculate the theoretical value of a three-month call option at $45 if the underlying stock is selling for $50 and has a variance of .36. The risk-free rate is 6 percent.

Fig. 5.3

```
┌─────────────────────────────────────────────────────┐
│           Data For Option Price Calculation          │
│                                                       │
│                 Stock Price ($):      50.000          │
│                                                       │
│               Strike Price  ($):      48.000          │
│                                                       │
│        Risk-free Interest Rate (%):    8.00           │
│                                                       │
│             Time to Expiry in Days:      90           │
│                                                       │
│     Volatility (Sigma) in decimals:    0.50           │
│                                                       │
└─────────────────────────────────────────────────────┘
```

     Please hit the <ENTER> key after entering data in each field

┌─────────────┐
│ Edit Input │   Show Results
└─────────────┘

*Problem from *Investments: Analysis, Selection and Management* by Edward A. Moses and John M. Cheney. © 1989 by West Publishing Company. Reprinted with permission from West Publishing Company.

Fig. 5.4

```
┌─────────────────────────────────────────────────┐
│                                                   │
│           Results of Option Calculations          │
│              (Black-Scholes Model)                │
│                                                   │
│   Call Price ($):  6.40      Put Price ($):  3.47 │
│                                                   │
│              Call Option Parameters               │
│                                                   │
│        Delta:    0.644      Theta:   -28.424      │
│                                                   │
│        Lambda:  10.599      Gamma:     0.034      │
│                                                   │
└─────────────────────────────────────────────────┘
```

```
┌──────────────┐
│ Print Results │   Edit Input     New Input     Hybrid Sec. Menu
└──────────────┘
```

The problem can be solved as follows:

$$d_1 = (ln(50/45) + (0.06 + 0.36/2) \times 0.25)/(\sqrt{0.25} \times \sqrt{0.36})$$
$$= 0.5512$$
$$d_2 = 0.5512 - \sqrt{0.36} \times \sqrt{0.25}$$
$$= 0.2512$$
$$P_c = 50 \times 0.7088 - 45 \times 0.9851 \times 0.5987$$
$$= \$8.90$$

To calculate the price of the call using the software, enter the following data:

Stock price	= 50
Striking price	= 45
Risk-free Rate of Return	= 6
Time to expiry	= 3 months
Volatility (sigma) in decimals	= 0.6 ($\sqrt{0.36}$)

When the variables are entered on the Data For Option Price Calculations screen, it will appear as in Figure 5.5. Highlight **Show Results** and press the ⟨**Enter**⟩ key and the Results of Option Calculations screen will appear. The solution is shown in Figure 5.6.

Sample Problem

Use the Black-Scholes formula to find the value of a call option on the following stock:

Time to maturity	= 6 months
Standard deviation	= 50% per year
Exercise Price	= $50
Stock Price	= $50
Interest rate	= 10% per year*

*Problem from *Investments* by Zvi Bodie, Alex Kane, and Alan J. Marcus. © 1989 by Richard D. Irwin. Reprinted with permission from Richard D. Irwin.

Fig. 5.5

```
┌──────────────────────────────────────────────────────────┐
│ ┌──────────────────────────────────────────────────────┐ │
│ │         Data For Option Price Calculation            │ │
│ │                                                      │ │
│ │              Stock Price ($):      50.000            │ │
│ │                                                      │ │
│ │             Strike Price  ($):     45.000            │ │
│ │                                                      │ │
│ │  Risk-free Interest Rate (%):       6.00             │ │
│ │                                                      │ │
│ │        Time to Expiry in Days:        90             │ │
│ │                                                      │ │
│ │  Volatility (Sigma) in decimals:    0.60             │ │
│ └──────────────────────────────────────────────────────┘ │
└──────────────────────────────────────────────────────────┘
```

Please hit the <ENTER> key after entering data in each field

| Edit Input | Show Results

The following steps can be used to solve the problem:

$$d_1 = (ln(1) + (0.10 + 0.25/2) \times 0.5)/(0.5 \times \sqrt{0.50})$$
$$= 0.3182 \qquad \text{(Nearest number from the table)}$$
$$d_2 = 0.3182 - 0.5 \times 0.50$$
$$= -0.035349$$
$$P_c = 50 \times 0.6155 - 50 \times 0.9512 \times 0.4925$$
$$= \$7.35 \qquad \text{(Approximate price of the call option)}$$

The following data need to be entered to find the price of the call option using the software:

Stock price   = 50
Striking price   = 50
Risk-free Rate of Return   = 10
Time to expiry   = 182
Volatility (sigma) in decimals   = 0.5

Fig. 5.6

```
┌──────────────────────────────────────────────────────────┐
│ ┌──────────────────────────────────────────────────────┐ │
│ │            Results of Option Calculations            │ │
│ │                (Black-Scholes Model)                 │ │
│ │                                                      │ │
│ │   Call Price ($):   8.86      Put Price ($):   3.20  │ │
│ │                                                      │ │
│ │              Call Option Parameters                  │ │
│ │                                                      │ │
│ │       Delta:   0.710          Theta:   -30.081       │ │
│ │                                                      │ │
│ │       Lambda: 11.537          Gamma:    0.031        │ │
│ └──────────────────────────────────────────────────────┘ │
└──────────────────────────────────────────────────────────┘
```

| Print Results | Edit Input   New Input   Hybrid Sec. Menu

Fig. 5.7

```
┌─────────────────────────────────────────────────────────┐
│                                                         │
│           Data For Option Price Calculation            │
│                                                         │
│                 Stock Price ($):      50.000           │
│                                                         │
│                Strike Price  ($):     50.000           │
│                                                         │
│        Risk-free Interest Rate (%):    10.00           │
│                                                         │
│             Time to Expiry in Days:      182           │
│                                                         │
│        Volatility (Sigma) in decimals:  0.50           │
│                                                         │
└─────────────────────────────────────────────────────────┘
```

Please hit the <ENTER> key after entering data in each field

┌──────────────┐
│ Edit Input   │   Show Results
└──────────────┘

Enter the above data in the Data For Option Price Calculations screen. The figures will appear as in Figure 5.7. Highlight **Show Results** and press the ⟨**Enter**⟩ key and the Results of Option Calculations screen will appear. The solution is shown in Figure 5.8.

This completes the discussion of call option pricing submodule. To continue, move the highlight bar to **Option Menu** and press ⟨**Enter**⟩. Now move the highlight bar to **Put-Call Parity Theorem — Put Price** and press the ⟨**Enter**⟩ key.

PUT-CALL PARITY THEOREM

The market prices of a put and a call option on a stock, with the same exercise price and maturity date, are related to each other. The put-call parity theorem expresses this relationship between the prices on a put and a call. If the parity relationship is violated, an arbitrage situation will exist providing

Fig. 5.8

```
┌─────────────────────────────────────────────────────────┐
│                                                         │
│                Results of Option Calculations           │
│                    (Black-Scholes Model)                │
│                                                         │
│    Call Price ($):  8.12      Put Price ($):   5.69    │
│                                                         │
│                Call Option Parameters                   │
│                                                         │
│         Delta:     0.625      Theta:    -26.818        │
│                                                         │
│         Lambda:   14.815      Gamma:      0.024        │
│                                                         │
└─────────────────────────────────────────────────────────┘
```

┌──────────────┐
│ Print Results │   Edit Input   New Input   Hybrid Sec. Menu
└──────────────┘

the investor with an opportunity of making riskless profits. The equation for the put-call parity theorem is:

$$P_p = P_c + Ee^{-R_fT} - S$$

The user must keep in mind that this model as well as the Black-Scholes option pricing model applies only to European options on stocks which pay no cash dividends.

To access this submodule, highlight **Put-Call Parity Theorem – Put Price (or Call Price)** in the **Analysis of Hybrid Securities** menu and press the ⟨**Enter**⟩ key. This will bring up the data entry screen for the submodule. The procedure for solving a problem for the put option price is identical to the procedure for solving for a call price. The guidelines for data entry discussed in the previous submodule also apply here.

Sample Problem

In February 1988, Gid Gardner sold a September 55 call on Concord Corp. stock for $4.375 per share and simultaneously bought a September 55 put on the same stock for $6 per share. At the time, Treasury bills coming due in September were priced to yield 12.6 percent and Concord stock sold for $53 per share. What value would putcall parity suggest was appropriate for the Concord put?*

To solve for the put price, the following calculation is needed:

$$P_p = 4.375 + 55 \times 0.929136 - 53$$
$$= \$2.48$$

To find the suggested put price, use the following data:

Call Price	= 4.375
Strike Price of the Option	= 55
Risk-free Interest Rate	= 12.6
Time to Expiry in Days	= 210 (7 months)
Current Market Price of the Stock	= 53

Enter these data in the input screen. It will appear as shown in Figure 5.9. Highlight **Show Results** and press ⟨**Enter**⟩ and the Put Price based on Put-Call Parity Theorem screen will appear. This is shown in Figure 5.10.

Move the highlight bar to **New Input** and press ⟨**Enter**⟩ to continue working problems in this area.

Sample Problem

A call option on XYZ Corp. expiring in 45 days with a strike price of $30 currently sell for $3.25. The XYZ stock is trading at $33.75 and the risk-free

---

*Problem from *Investments* by William F. Sharpe and Gordon J. Alexander. © 1990 by Prentice Hall, Inc. Reprinted with permission from Prentice Hall, Inc.

Fig. 5.9

```
┌─────────────────────────────────────────────────────────┐
│                                                           │
│                  Put-Call Parity Theorem                  │
│                                                           │
│                       Call Price ($):    4.375            │
│                                                           │
│          Strike Price of the Option ($):  55.000          │
│                                                           │
│            Risk-Free Interest Rate ($):   12.60           │
│                                                           │
│         Days to Expiration of the Option:    210          │
│                                                           │
│   Current Market Price of the Stock ($):   53.00          │
│                                                           │
└─────────────────────────────────────────────────────────┘
```

```
       Please hit the <ENTER> key after entering data in each field
     ┌──────────────┐
     │  Edit Input  │                              Show Results
     └──────────────┘
```

rate is 8 percent. What should the put option on the stock with the same strike price and maturity date sell for?

$$\text{The put price} = 3.25 + 35 \times .9902 - 33.75$$
$$= \$4.16$$

Enter the following data to find the put price using the software:

Call Price	= 3.25
Strike Price of the Option	= 35
Risk-free Interest	= 8
Time to Expiry in Days	= 45
Current Market Price of the Stock	= 33.75

On entering these data, the input screen should appear as in Figure 5.11. Highlight **Show Results** and press ⟨**Enter**⟩ and the Put Price based on Put-Call Parity Theorem screen will appear. This is shown in Figure 5.12.

Fig. 5.10

```
┌─────────────────────────────────────────────────────────┐
│                                                           │
│       Put Price Based on Put-Call Parity Theorem          │
│                                                           │
│    1.  Call Price ($):                         4.38       │
│                                                           │
│    2.  Present Value of Strike Price ($):     51.10       │
│                                                           │
│    3.  Current Market Price ($):              53.00       │
│                                                           │
│    Put Price = (1) + (2) - (3) =               2.48       │
│                                                           │
└─────────────────────────────────────────────────────────┘
```

```
┌────────────────┐
│  Print Results │   Edit Input      New Input      Hybrid Sec. Menu
└────────────────┘
```

Fig. 5.11

```
┌─────────────────────────────────────────────────────────┐
│ ┌─────────────────────────────────────────────────────┐ │
│ │            Put-Call Parity Theorem                  │ │
│ │                                                     │ │
│ │                    Call Price ($):     3.250        │ │
│ │                                                     │ │
│ │    Strike Price of the Option ($):    35.000        │ │
│ │                                                     │ │
│ │        Risk-Free Interest Rate ($):    8.00         │ │
│ │                                                     │ │
│ │     Days to Expiration of the Option:    45         │ │
│ │                                                     │ │
│ │  Current Market Price of the Stock ($):  33.75      │ │
│ │                                                     │ │
│ └─────────────────────────────────────────────────────┘ │
└─────────────────────────────────────────────────────────┘
```

Please hit the <ENTER> key after entering data in each field

Edit Input   Show Results

IMPLIED VOLATILITY

One important variable affecting the price of a call option is the volatility of returns from the security underlying the option. It is measured by the standard deviation of the annualized continuously compounded rates of return from the underlying security. A large number of historical returns from the security are needed to estimate this variable. However, in an actively traded stock and options market, investors' perception about the security keeps changing because of new information and, therefore, the volatility estimated from historical data has questionable value. One way of resolving this dilemma is to measure the volatility implied in the market price of a call option. This submodule calculates the implied volatility from the Black-Scholes option pricing model using a trial and error procedure. This measure can then be applied to other options to determine the intrinsic value of those options. Research has shown that the best estimates of the implied standard deviation are determined from "at-the-money" options.

Fig. 5.12

```
┌─────────────────────────────────────────────────────────┐
│                                                         │
│        Put Price Based on Put-Call Parity Theorem       │
│                                                         │
│    1.   Call Price ($):                         3.25    │
│                                                         │
│    2.   Present Value of Strike Price ($):     34.65    │
│                                                         │
│    3.   Current Market Price ($):              33.75    │
│                                                         │
│    Put Price = (1) + (2) - (3) =                4.10    │
│                                                         │
└─────────────────────────────────────────────────────────┘
```

Print Results   Edit Input   New Input   Hybrid Sec. Menu

To access this submodule, highlight the choice **Implied Volatility** in the **Analysis of Hybrid Securities** menu and hit the ⟨**Enter**⟩ key. This will bring up the data entry screen for the submodule.

Sample Problem

The following information on a call option expiring in 30 days on the S&P 500 Index is available:

Call Price	= $6.00
Strike Price	= 375
Current Value of the Index	= 371.07
Risk-free Interest Rate	= 5.00%

Calculate the volatility of the S&P 500 Index implied in the option price.

The solution has to be determined by a trial and error process. It is preferable, therefore, to rely on the computer to solve this problem, with the following input data:

Stock Price	= 371.07
Strike Price	= 375
Risk-free Interest Rate	= 5.00
Time to Expiry in Days	= 30
Call Option Price	= 6

The completed data input screen is shown in Figure 5.13. Highlight the choice **Show Results** and press the ⟨**Enter**⟩ key. This will bring up the solution to the problem, which shown in Figure 5.14.

To access the next submodule, highlight the choice **Hybrid Sec. Menu** press the ⟨**Enter**⟩ key. This will bring up the main menu in the **Analysis of Hybrid Securities** module.

Fig. 5.13

```
┌──────────────────────────────────────────────────┐
│        Data For Implied Volatility Calculation     │
│           Stock Price ($):    371.070              │
│          Strike Price ($):    375.000              │
│   Risk-free Interest Rate (%):    5.00             │
│         Time to Expiry in Days:     30             │
│        Call Option Price ($):     6.00             │
│                                                    │
└──────────────────────────────────────────────────┘
```

Please hit the <ENTER> key after entering data in each field

```
┌──────────────┐
│  Edit Input  │                              Show Results
└──────────────┘
```

Fig. 5.14

```
┌─────────────────────────────────────────────────────┐
│                                                       │
│      Results of Implied Volatility Calculations       │
│                                                       │
│   Volatility (Sigma) is calculated by trial and error │
│              (Based on Black-Scholes Model)           │
│                                                       │
│      Implied Volatility (Sigma):   0.168              │
│                                                       │
└─────────────────────────────────────────────────────┘
```

┌──────────────────┐
│ Print Results   │   Edit Input   New Input   Hybrid Sec. Menu
└──────────────────┘

CONVERTIBLE BONDS

A convertible bond is a bond which offers the owner of the bond an option to exchange the bond for a predetermined number of shares of common stock. The exchange is based on the conversion ratio which specifies the number of shares to be received for each bond. The conversion price of the common stock is equal to the face value of the bond (usually $1,000) divided by the conversion ratio. At the time of the bond issue, the conversion ratio is set such that the conversion price is 15 to 25 percent higher than the current market price of the common stock. It is expected that the stock price will increase over time due to the higher earning from the new investments undertaken by the firm.

The market price of the convertible bond will be higher than the larger of the two values: the straight bond value and the conversion value (which is defined later in the section). This implies that there are premiums which an investor needs to analyze: the premium over the straight bond value and the premium over the conversion value of the bond.

As the market price of the stock exceeds the conversion price of the stock, the investor's decision about exchanging the bond for shares of common stock will depend upon the cash flow provided by owning the bond versus the cash flow from owning the shares of common stock. The cash flow from the bond is expressed by the current yield on the bond, while the cash flow from the stock is the dividend yield from the stock. The solution screen provides the user with all the above details for a convertible bond.

The following equations express the relationships discussed above:

$$V_d = I \times \text{PVIFA}_{K,n} + M \times \text{PVIF}_{K,n}$$
$$V_c = CR \times S$$

The premium of the market price over the straight bond value is calculated using the following equation:

$$X_d = \frac{V - V_d}{V_d}$$

The premium of the market value over the conversion value can be determined using the following formula:

$$X_c = \frac{V - V_c}{V_c}$$

To access the submodule, highlight **Convertible Bond Analysis** in the **Analysis of Hybrid Securities** menu and press the ⟨**Enter**⟩ key. This will bring up the data entry screen for the submodule.

Sample Problem

Assume that you just paid $1,200 for a convertible bond that carries a 7.5 percent coupon and has 15 years to maturity. The bond can be converted into 24 shares of common stock which are now trading at $50 a share. Find the bond investment value, given that comparable nonconvertible bonds are presently selling to yield 9 percent.*

The problem solution requires only the investment value of the bond (i.e., the straight bond value). This is the value of the bond based on a 9 percent yield-to-maturity. The solution is similar to the illustrative examples in the **Bond Price—Interest Date** submodule and will not be presented here. The **Convertible Bond Analysis** submodule, however, will provide a number of details about the bond. To get the software solution to this problem, enter the following data (note that the input is divided in two different screens):

Screen 1   (Straight Bond Data)

Face Value	= 1000
Coupon Rate	= 7.50
Number of Coupon Payments Remaining	= 15
Yield-to-maturity on Similar Risk Bonds	= 9
Number of Coupon Payments per Year	= 1 (Assumed)

The data input screen with the above data entered is shown in Figure 5.15. Highlight the choice **Next Screen** and press the ⟨**Enter**⟩ key to bring up the second input screen.

Screen 2   (Conversion Data)

Conversion Ratio	= 24
Cash Dividend per Share	= 0 (No Information)
Market Price of the Stock	= 50
Market Price of the Bond	= 1200

*Problem from *Fundamentals of Investments* by Lawrence J. Gitman and Michael D. Joehnk. © 1990 by Lawrence J. Gitman and Michael D. Joehnk. Reprinted with Permission from HarperCollins Publishers.

Fig. 5.15

```
┌─────────────────────────────────────────────────────────┐
│                    Convertible Bond Data                 │
│                                                          │
│                        Face Value ($):     1000.00       │
│                                                          │
│                       Coupon Rate (%):        7.50       │
│                                                          │
│          Number of Coupon Pmts Remaining:       15       │
│                                                          │
│     Yld. to Mat. on Similar Risk Bonds (%):     9.00     │
│                                                          │
│           Number of Coupon Pmts per Year:        1       │
│                                                          │
└─────────────────────────────────────────────────────────┘
```

Please hit <ENTER> key after entering data in each field

┌──────────────┐
│ Edit Input │   Show Results
└──────────────┘

Enter the above data in the second input screen. This screen is shown in Figure 5.16. Highlight **Show Results** and press ⟨**Enter**⟩ to bring up the first solution screen. The solution is shown in Figure 5.17. Repeat the process to bring up the second solution screen which is shown in Figure 5.18.

    This concludes the discussion of the submodules in the **Analysis of Hybrid Securities** module. Highlight the choice **Hybrid Sec. Menu** on the menu bar and press the ⟨**Enter**⟩ key to go back to the main menu in the module. Exit from the module and the control is passed to the **Investment Problem Menu**. Any other module can be accessed from here.

Fig. 5.16

```
┌─────────────────────────────────────────────────────────┐
│          Convertible Bond Data (Continued)               │
│                                                          │
│        Conversion Rate (# of Shares):     24.00          │
│                                                          │
│          Cash Dividend per Share ($):      0.00          │
│                                                          │
│         Market Price of the Stock ($):    50.00          │
│                                                          │
│    Market Price of the Conv. Bond ($):   1200.00         │
│                                                          │
└─────────────────────────────────────────────────────────┘
```

Please hit the <ENTER> key after entering data in each field

┌──────────────┐
│ Edit Input │   Show Results
└──────────────┘

Fig. 5.17

```
          Convertible Bond Analysis

  1.  Discount Rate Used(%):                    9.00

  2.  Present Value of Coupons($):            604.55

  3.  Present Value of the Principal($):      274.54

  4.  The Sum of (2) & (3) Equals
      Investment Value of the Bond($):        879.09

  5.  Conversion Value of the Bond($):       1200.00
```

    Print Results   More Results

Fig. 5.18

```
          Convertible Bond Analysis (Contd.)

   Market Premium over Conversion Value (%):    0.00

   Market Premium over Investment Value (%):   36.50

   Conversion Parity Price of the Stock ($):   50.00

   Current Yield on the Stock (%):              0.00

   Current Yield on the Bond (%):               6.25

   Breakeven Period (Years):                    0.00
```

   Print Results   Edit Input   New Input   Hybrid Sec. Menu

6 *Portfolio Theory*

Portfolio theory plays an extremely important role in modern investment analysis. The development of portfolio theory has led to revolutionary changes in the practice of investments. Several new types of investment instruments such as mutual funds and index funds owe their existence to portfolio theory. The contribution of this theory has been judged to be very important not only to the theory of investments, but also to the broader discipline of economics. Two pioneers, Professor Harry Markovitz and Professor William F. Sharpe, who led the way in developing this theory were awarded the 1990 Nobel Prize in economics.

A portfolio can be defined as a combination of two or more assets. It can be easily shown that a combination of two risky assets under proper circumstances would lead to a portfolio with better risk-return characteristics compared to the two individual assets. The *risk* of an asset is defined as the standard deviation of returns from the asset. The calculation of the portfolio standard deviation involves a lot of number crunching, even for a two-asset portfolio. The complexity increases as the number of assets in the portfolio increases. The portfolio theory module in **Investment Problem Solver** is designed to reduce the number of calculations in portfolio analysis.

The study of portfolio theory also involves various statistical concepts like expected values, standard deviations, covariances, and correlation coefficients. Calculations of these measures become easy with the help of this module.

The **Portfolio Theory** module in **Investment Problem Solver** includes the following submodules:

1. Risk Return Analysis
2. Covariance/Correlation
3. Beta Estimation
4. Portfolio Analysis
5. Security Market Line
6. Minimum Risk Portfolio
7. Portfolio Performance Evaluation

The first submodule accepts security data to provide the expected return and the standard deviation of the returns from the security. The input data can be in the form of historical data or a probability distribution of returns.

Submodule 2 estimates the covariance or the correlation coefficient between the returns from two securities. Once again, the input data can be in the form of historical returns or a probability distribution of returns.

The next submodule is designed to calculate the beta of a security by regressing the returns from the security against those of the market portfolio. Up to 15 observations can be used in the regression analysis. The submodule also provides results on arithmetic and geometric average returns, and the standard deviation of returns for each asset in question. The regression results provide data about alpha, beta, the R^2 statistic and the standard errors of alpha and beta. The respective t-statistics for alpha and beta can be estimated from this information.

The expected return and the standard deviation of expected returns of a security can be calculated using the fourth submodule. As before, input data can be either in the form of historical returns or a probability distribution of returns. This submodule can accommodate portfolios of up to five securities.

The next submodule can provide the equilibrium expected returns from a security based on the Security Market Line (SML).

The sixth submodule allows the user to determine the minimum risk portfolio for a two-security portfolio. The required inputs are the standard deviations of returns for the individual securities and the correlation coefficient between those returns.

The last submodule in this section calculates the reward to variability (Sharpe Index) and reward to volatility (Treynor Index) ratios for up to two portfolios.

The rest of this chapter will illustrate the use of this module by solving a number of problems on the topic of portfolio theory. These problems are selected from some of the leading textbooks on investments and portfolio analysis.

GETTING STARTED

To access the **Portfolio Theory** module from the main menu, highlight the choice **Portfolio Theory** in the menu using either the space bar or the arrow keys. Press the ⟨**Enter**⟩ key to indicate your choice. This will bring up the **Portfolio Theory** menu on the screen, offering a choice among seven different submodules. Once again, any one of these seven submodules can be accessed using a procedure similar to the one described previously.

NOTATION

The following symbols will be used in the various formulae in this chapter:

R_{it} = Return from asset i in the time period t

R_p = Expected return from a portfolio

σ_i = Standard deviation of returns from security i

α = The intercept term in regression analysis

B_i = Beta of security i

W_i = Fraction of portfolio invested in security i

R_f = Rate of return on the risk-free asset

R_m = Rate of return on the market portfolio

P_i = The probability of occurrence of the event i

σ_{ij} = Covariance between returns from security i with those of security j

ρ_{ij} = Correlation coefficient between returns form security i and those from security j

$E(R_i)$ = Expected return from security i.

In formulae involving summation, i or t will be used as the index variable depending upon the variable over which the sum is calculated.

RISK RETURN ANALYSIS

The most important assumption underlying the portfolio theory is that when investors make investment decisions, they only consider two characteristics of the security in question, namely, the expected return from the security and the risk of the security. It is important, therefore, that students of investments be able to determine these two characteristics for a security given pertinent data. The preferred procedure is to determine these characteristics based on future expectations expressed in the form of a probability distribution of returns from the security. In the absence of such information, the expected returns and the risk of a security may be based on past data (i.e., the historical returns from the security). The **Risk Return Analysis** submodule is designed to accept data in either form.

The following formulae are employed in calculating the risk return measure from a probability distribution:

$$E(R) = \sum_{i=1}^{n} R_i \times P_i$$

and

$$\sigma = \sqrt{\sum_{i=1}^{n} P_i \times (R_i - E(R))^2}$$

where n is the number of possible states in the probability distribution.

The formulae for estimating the two parameters from the historical returns are given below:

$$E(r) = \frac{\sum_{t=1}^{T} R_t}{T}$$

and

$$\sigma = \sqrt{\frac{\sum_{t=1}^{T} (R_t - E(R))^2}{(T - 1)}}$$

where T is the number time periods over which returns data are available.

To enter the **Risk Return** module, highlight that choice in the **Portfolio Theory** menu, and press the ⟨**Enter**⟩ key. This action will bring up the data entry screen. Appropriate data are then entered to obtain the solution for the problem.

Sample Problem

The following are the monthly rates of return for Anheuser-Busch and General Motors during a six-month period:

Month	Anheuser-Busch	General Motors
1	.04	.07
2	.03	−.02
3	−.07	−.10
4	.12	.15
5	−.02	−.06
6	.05	.02

Compute the following:

a. The mean monthly rates of return for each stock; and

b. The standard deviation for each stock.*

This problem can be solved as follows:

Mean monthly rate for A − B = (.04 + .03 − .07 + .12 − .02 + .05)/6
           = .025 or 2.5%

Similarly,

Mean monthly rate for G.M. = (0.07 − 0.02 − 0.10 + 0.15 − 0.06 + 0.02)/6
           = 0.01 or 1%

Standard deviation of returns for A − B

$= \sqrt{((0.04 - 0.025)^2 + (0.03 - 0.025)^2 + \ldots + (0.05 - 0.025)^2)/6}$
$= 0.0591$

And,

Standard deviation of returns for G.M.

$= \sqrt{((0.07 - 0.01)^2 + \ldots + \ldots + (0.02 - 0.01)^2)/6} = 0.0787$

*Problem from *Investments* by Frank K. Reilly. © 1986 by CBS College Publishing. Reprinted with permission from The Dryden Press.

The software solution to this problem can be obtained by entering the following data (data for the two stocks should be entered separately):

Number of Data Points = 6   (On the first screen)

The input data are in the form of historical returns. Therefore, after entering the above data, highlight **Input Historical Data** in the menu bar and press the ⟨**Enter**⟩ key. This will bring up a data input table on the screen. Enter the six monthly returns in percentages in the appropriate places as follows:

	Anheuser-Busch
Obs. # 1 =	4
Obs. # 2 =	3
Obs. # 3 =	−7
Obs. # 4 =	12
Obs. # 5 =	−2
Obs. # 6 =	5

After all data have been entered (as shown in Figure 6.1), the menu appears at the bottom of the screen offering two options: **Edit Input** and **Show Results**. After making sure that all data have been entered correctly, highlight the choice **Show Results** and press ⟨**Enter**⟩. This will bring up the solution screen, which is shown in Figure 6.2.

To obtain the solution for G.M., highlight the choice **Edit Input** in the menu bar and press the ⟨**Enter**⟩ key. Enter the following returns data for G.M.:

Number of Data Points = 6   (In screen 1)

	G.M.
Obs. # 1 =	7
Obs. # 2 =	−2
Obs. # 3 =	−10
Obs. # 4 =	15
Obs. # 5 =	−6
Obs. # 6 =	2

Fig. 6.1

```
┌─────────────────────────────────────────────────────────┐
│   Historical Returns Data for Asssets/Portfolios         │
│                                                          │
│   Asset/Portfolio Return in Period 1 (%):    4.00        │
│   Asset/Portfolio Return in Period 2 (%):    3.00        │
│   Asset/Portfolio Return in Period 3 (%):   -7.00        │
│   Asset/Portfolio Return in Period 4 (%):   12.00        │
│   Asset/Portfolio Return in Period 5 (%):   -2.00        │
│   Asset/Portfolio Return in Period 6 (%):    5.00        │
│                                                          │
└─────────────────────────────────────────────────────────┘
```

Please hit the <ENTER> key after entering data in each field

┌─────────────────┐
│   Edit Input   │   Show Results
└─────────────────┘

Fig. 6.2

```
┌─────────────────────────────────────────────────────┐
│ ┌─────────────────────────────────────────────────┐ │
│ │     Risk-Return Analysis for the Asset/Portfolio │ │
│ │                                                   │ │
│ │  Expected Return on the Asset/Portfolio:    2.50 │ │
│ │                                                   │ │
│ │  Std. Dev. of the Asset/Portfolio Returns (%): 5.91 │ │
│ └─────────────────────────────────────────────────┘ │
└─────────────────────────────────────────────────────┘
```

┌─────────────────┐
│ Print Results │   Edit Input   New Input   Portfolio Menu
└─────────────────┘

Highlight the choice **Show Results** and press the ⟨**Enter**⟩ key to bring up the solution for G.M.

To continue working problems in this submodule, highlight the choice **New Input** and press the ⟨**Enter**⟩ key.

Sample Problem

You have determined the following probability distribution for the returns from the common stock of ABC Corp. Calculate the expected return and the standard deviation of expected return from the stock.

Probability	Return
0.20	0.10
0.30	0.12
0.30	0.14
0.20	0.16

Applying the previous formulae, the solution to this problem is

Expected Return = $E(R)$

$E(R) = 0.20 \times 0.10 + 0.30 \times 0.12 + 0.30 \times 0.14 + 0.20 \times 0.16$

$\quad = 0.13$ or 13%

$\quad = \sqrt{(0.20 \times (0.10 - 0.13)^2 + \ldots + \ldots + (0.20 \times (0.16 - 0.13)^2)}$

$\quad = 0.0205$ or 2.05%

For the software solution, enter the following data in the first input screen:

Number of Data Points   = 4

In this sample problem, the stock data are provided in the form of a probability distribution. Therefore, after the above data are entered, highlight **Input Probability Dist.** and press the ⟨**Enter**⟩ key to bring up the next input screen. Enter the following data in the second input screen:

Probability	Return
20	10
30	12
30	14
20	16

Fig. 6.3

```
┌──────────────────────────────────────────────────────────────┐
│  Probability Distribution of Asset/Portfolio Returns           │
│                                                                │
│  1. Return (%):   10.000    Probability (%):    20.00          │
│  2. Return (%):   12.000    Probability (%):    30.00          │
│  3. Return (%):   14.000    Probability (%):    30.00          │
│  4. Return (%):   16.000    Probability (%):    20.00          │
└──────────────────────────────────────────────────────────────┘
```

Please hit the <ENTER> key after entering data in each field

| Edit Input | Show Results

The completed data entry screen is shown in Figure 6.3. After ensuring that all data are entered correctly, highlight the choice **Show Results** in the menu bar and press the ⟨**Enter**⟩ key. This will bring up the solution shown in Figure 6.4.

Sample Problem

A stock that currently pays no dividend is selling for $100. The possible prices for which the stock might sell at the year-end with the associated probabilities are:

Year-end Price	Probability
90	0.10
100	0.20
110	0.40
120	0.20
130	0.10

a. Calculate the expected rate of return by year-end; and

b. Calculate the standard deviation of expected rate of return.

To solve this problem, the rates of return at different prices must be calculated with the beginning price of $100.

Fig. 6.4

```
┌──────────────────────────────────────────────────────────────┐
│     Risk-Return Analysis for the Asset/Portfolio               │
│                                                                │
│  Expected Return on the Asset/Portfolio:        13.00          │
│                                                                │
│  Std. Dev. of the Asset/Portfolio Returns (%): 2.05            │
│                                                                │
└──────────────────────────────────────────────────────────────┘
```

| Print Results | Edit Input   New Input   Portfolio Menu

Year-end Price	Rate of Return
90	-0.10
100	0.00
110	0.10
120	0.20
130	0.30

Next, using the above formula

Expected Rate of Return

$$= 0.10 \times (-0.10) + 0.20 \times 0.00 + 0.40 \times 0.10$$
$$+ 0.20 \times 0.20 + 0.10 \times 0.30$$
$$= .10 \text{ or } 10\%$$

Variance of Expected Returns $= (-0.10 - 0.10)^2 \times 0.10 +$
$(0.00 - 0.10)^2 \times 0.20 + (0.10 - 0.10)^2 \times 0.40 +$
$(0.20 - 0.10)^2 \times 0.20 + (0.30 - 0.10)^2 \times 0.10$
$= 0.012$

Standard Deviation of Expected Returns $= 0.1095$ or 10.95%

The software solution to the problem can be found by entering the following data in data entry screen:

Number of Data Points $= 5$ (In the first screen)

Obs. #	Rate of Return (%)	Probability (%)
1	-10	10
2	0	20
3	10	40
4	20	20
5	30	10

The second data entry screen will appear as shown in Figure 6.5. Highlight **Input Probability Dist.** and press the ⟨**Enter**⟩ key. The required solution will appear as in Figure 6.6.

The discussion and the illustrative examples in the **Risk Return Analysis** submodule are now complete. To access another submodule in the **Portfolio Theory** module, highlight **Portfolio Menu** in the menu bar and press the

Fig. 6.5

```
┌─────────────────────────────────────────────────────────────┐
│   Probability Distribution of Asset/Portfolio Returns        │
│                                                              │
│   1. Return (%):   -10.000    Probability (%):    10.00      │
│   2. Return (%):     0.000    Probability (%):    20.00      │
│   3. Return (%):    10.000    Probability (%):    40.00      │
│   4. Return (%):    20.000    Probability (%):    20.00      │
│   5. Return (%):    30.000    Probability (%):    10.00      │
│                                                              │
└─────────────────────────────────────────────────────────────┘
```

```
    Please hit the <ENTER> key after entering data in each field
   ┌─────────────────┐
   │  Edit Input     │                              Show Results
   └─────────────────┘
```

Fig. 6.6

```
┌──────────────────────────────────────────────────────────┐
│      Risk-Return Analysis for the Asset/Portfolio         │
│                                                            │
│   Expected Return on the Asset/Portfolio:        10.00     │
│                                                            │
│   Std. Dev. of the Asset/Portfolio Returns (%): 10.95      │
│                                                            │
└──────────────────────────────────────────────────────────┘
```

```
┌─────────────────┐
│  Print Results  │    Edit Input      New Input     Portfolio Menu
└─────────────────┘
```

⟨**Enter**⟩ key. The control will be handed over to the main menu of the module, from where any other submodule can be accessed.

COVARIANCE AND CORRELATION ANALYSIS

The statistical concepts of covariance and correlation coefficient play an important role in the determination of portfolio risk. The covariance between two variable measures the degree to which the two variables "move together" over time. A positive covariance indicates that the two variables, on the average, move in the same direction over time. A negative covariance will suggest that the two variable tend to move in opposite direction over time.

In portfolio theory, it is the covariance between the returns from two securities which determines the benefits of diversification in the form of reduced portfolio risk. Covariance between the returns of two securities will depend upon the variances of the security returns and the comovement of the returns. If two securities have a negative covariance, then they will yield a portfolio with a significantly lower risk.

The covariance between the returns of two securities can be estimated either from a probability distribution or from historical returns data. The formula to obtain the covariance from a probability distribution is:

$$\sigma_{ab} = \sum_{i=1}^{n} P_i \left[R_{ai} - E(R_a) \right] \left[R_{bi} - E(R_b) \right]$$

The formula for covariance from historical returns data is as follows:

$$\sigma_{ab} = \frac{\sum_{t=1}^{T} \left[R_{at} - E(R_a) \right] \left[R_{bt} - E(R_b) \right]}{T}$$

Since the covariance of returns from two securities will depend to a large extent on the variances of the two return streams, it can be very large for volatile securities and small for securities which are stable. Interpreting covariances can therefore be rather difficult. The correlation coefficient standardizes the covariances by removing the effect of the individual variances. The resulting coefficient always lies between -1 and $+1$, thus yielding a much better measure for comparative purposes. The correlation coefficient between the return streams of two securities A and B, ρ_{ab} can be calculated as:

$$\rho_{ab} = \frac{\sigma_{ab}}{\sigma_a \sigma_b}$$

The input data for problems on this topic may either be in the form of a joint probability distribution or in the form of historical observations. The user is allowed to enter the input data in either form.

To access the **Covariance/Correlation Analysis** submodule, highlight the choice in the **Portfolio Theory** menu and press ⟨**Enter**⟩. This will bring up the data entry screen for covariance/correlation analysis.

Sample Problem

The following problem will illustrate the use of the software in calculating covariances and correlation coefficients on an "ex ante" basis (i.e., from probability distribution data).

Calculate the covariance and the correlation coefficient between the returns of stock I and stock J, from the following information:

State	Condition of Economy	Probability (%)	Return on I	Return on J
1	Good	30	20	15
2	Fair	40	15	12
3	Poor	30	10	9

To solve this problem, the student will have to calculate the following:

$$E(R_I) = .3 \times 20 + .40 \times 15 + .30 \times 10$$
$$= 15\%$$
$$E(R_J) = 12\%$$
$$\sigma_I = \sqrt{[0.30 \times (20 - 15)^2 + 0.40 \times (15 - 15)^2}$$
$$\overline{+ 0.30 \times (10 - 15)^2]}$$
$$= 3.87\%$$
$$\sigma_J = 2.32\%$$
$$\sigma_{IJ} = 0.30 \times (20 - 15)(15 - 12) + 0.4 \times (15 - 15)(12 - 12)$$
$$+ 0.3 \times (10 - 15)(9 - 12)$$
$$= 9.00$$
$$\rho_{IJ} = 9/(3.87 \times 2.32)$$
$$= 1.00 \quad \text{(Difference is due to the rounding error)}$$

To solve this problem with the help of the software, enter the following data in the data entry screen:

Number of Data Points   = 3   (To be entered in screen 1)

The stock data, to be entered in the second screen, are in the form of a probability distribution. Therefore, highlight **Input Probability Dist.** in the menu bar and press the ⟨**Enter**⟩ key. This will bring up the suitable input screen for stock data.

Fig. 6.7

```
┌─────────────────────────────────────────────────────────┐
│ ┌───────────────────────────────────────────────────┐   │
│ │        Covariance/Correlation Analysis            │   │
│ │  #   Prob.(%) Return (%): Asset 1  Return (%): Asset 2 │
│ │  1    30.00      20.000              15.000        │   │
│ │  2    40.00      15.000              12.000        │   │
│ │  3    30.00      10.000               9.000        │   │
│ └───────────────────────────────────────────────────┘   │
└─────────────────────────────────────────────────────────┘
```

Please hit the <ENTER> key after entering data in each field

┌─────────────┐
│ Edit Input │   Show Results
└─────────────┘

		Rate of Return	
Obs. #	*Probability (%)*	*Asset 1*	*Asset 2*
1	30	20	15
2	40	15	12
3	30	10	9

After data entry, the second screen would appear as in Figure 6.7. Highlight the choice **Show Results** and press the ⟨**Enter**⟩ key. The solution screen, shown in Figure 6.8 will appear.

The determination of covariance and correlation coefficient based on historical data ("ex post") is explained in the following problem.

Sample Problem

Calculate the correlation coefficient and the covariance between the returns from the stock of Hartford Inc. and the market portfolio. The following information about the returns from these stocks is available:*

Fig. 6.8

```
┌──────────────────────────────────────────────────────────┐
│        Results of Covariance/Correlation Analysis        │
│                                                          │
│  Expected Return on Asset 1 (%):              15.00      │
│                                                          │
│  Expected Return on Asset 2 (%):              12.00      │
│                                                          │
│  Standard Deviation of Returns on Asset 1(%):  3.87      │
│                                                          │
│  Standard Deviation of Returns on Asset 2(%):  2.32      │
│                                                          │
│  Covariance between Returns-Asset 1 & Asset 2 (%%):  9.00 │
│                                                          │
│  Corr. Coeff. between Returns-Asset 1 & Asset 2(%%): 1.000 │
└──────────────────────────────────────────────────────────┘
```

┌───────────────┐
│ Print Results │   Edit Input   New Input   Portfolio Menu
└───────────────┘

*Problem from *Fundamentals of Investments* by Gordon J. Alexander and William F. Sharpe. © 1989 by Prentice Hall, Inc. Reprinted with permission from Prentice Hall, Inc.

Year	Hartford Inc. %	Market Portfolio %
1	8.1	8.0
2	3.0	0.0
3	5.3	14.9
4	1.0	5.0
5	−3.1	−4.1
6	−3.0	−8.9
7	5.0	10.1
8	3.2	5.0
9	1.2	1.5
10	1.3	2.4

The solution to the problem, based on the above formulae, is:

$$E(R_H) = (8.1 + 3.0 + \ldots + \ldots + \ldots + 1.3)/10$$
$$= 2.2\%$$
$$\sigma_H = 3.35\%$$
$$E(R_m) = (8.0 + 0.0 + \ldots + \ldots + \ldots + 2.4)/10$$
$$= 3.39\%$$
$$\sigma_m = 6.54\%$$
$$\sigma_{mH} = [(8.01 - 2.2)(8.0 - 3.39) + (3.0 - 2.2)(0.0 - 3.39) + \ldots +]/10$$
$$= 18.50$$

Finally, the correlation coefficient is

$$\rho_{mH} = 18.50/(6.54 \times 3.35)$$
$$= 0.844$$

The software solution needs the input of the following data:

Number of Observations   = 10   (In screen 1)

The stock data, to be entered in the second screen, are in the form of a historical returns. Therefore, highlight **Input Historical Data** in the menu bar and press the ⟨**Enter**⟩ key. This will bring up the suitable input screen for stock data.

Obs. #	Return on Stock	Return on Market
1	8.1	8.0
2	3.0	0.0
3	5.3	14.9
4	1.0	5.0
5	−3.1	−4.1
6	−3.0	−8.9
7	5.0	10.1
8	3.2	5.0
9	1.2	1.5
10	1.3	2.4

After data entry, the second screen will appear as in Figure 6.9. Highlight the choice **Show Results** and press the ⟨**Enter**⟩ key. The solution screen, shown in Figure 6.10, will appear.

Fig. 6.9

```
                  Covariance/Correlation Analysis
      Obs. #      Return (%): Asset 1      Return (%): Asset 2
        1                8.1                      8.0
        2                3.0                      0.0
        3                5.3                     14.9
        4                1.0                      5.0
        5               -3.1                     -4.1
        6               -3.0                     -8.9
        7                5.0                     10.1
        8                3.2                      5.0
        9                1.2                      1.5
       10                1.3                      2.4
```

Please hit the <ENTER> key after entering data in each field

Edit Input   Show Results

The discussion and the sample problems in this submodule are now complete. To access another submodule in the **Portfolio Analysis** module, highlight **Portfolio Menu** in the menu bar and press the ⟨**Enter**⟩ key. The control will be passed to the main menu of the module, from where the next submodule can be accessed.

BETA ESTIMATION

Whereas the standard deviation of returns from a security is a measure of its **total risk**, beta is a measure of the **systematic risk** of a security. In other words, beta measures that part of a security's risk which cannot be diversified away by forming a portfolio of securities.

Estimation of beta for the security i is usually based on the market model or the single factor model, presented below:

$$r_{it} = \alpha_i + B_i r_{mt} + \epsilon_t$$

Fig. 6.10

```
           Results of Covariance/Correlation Analysis

Expected Return on Asset 1 (%):                            2.20

Expected Return on Asset 2 (%):                            3.39

Standard Deviation of Returns on Asset 1(%):              3.35

Standard Deviation of Returns on Asset 2(%):              6.54

Covariance between Returns-Asset 1 & Asset 2 (%%): 18.50

Corr. Coeff. between Returns-Asset 1 & Asset 2(%%): 0.845
```

Print Results   Edit Input   New Input   Portfolio Menu

B_i, the slope coefficient in the above equation is the measure of the systematic risk (beta) of the security and it is calculated from the following equation:

$$B_i = \frac{\sigma_{im}}{\sigma_m^2}$$

Students are required to use regression analysis to determine beta of a stock from the above equation. Meaningful results can be obtained by selecting a data sample of more than 15 observations. Estimation of the beta coefficient, therefore, can involve a large number of calculations. The **Beta Estimation** submodule in **Investment Problem Solver** can reduce the task to that of a simple data entry. The submodule can accept data both as percentage returns and decimal returns.

The **submodule** can be accessed through the **Portfolio Theory** menu by highlighting the choice and pressing the ⟨**Enter**⟩ key. This action will bring up the data entry screen for beta estimation problems.

Sample Problem

In the following table you are presented with 10 years of return data for Hartford Inc. and for the market portfolio. Plot the returns of Hartford and the market on a graph. From the graph only, compute an estimate of the beta of Hartford stock.*

Year	Hartford Inc. (%)	Market Portfolio (%)
1	8.1	8.0
2	3.0	0.0
3	5.3	14.9
4	1.0	5.0
5	−3.1	−4.1
6	−3.0	−8.9
7	5.0	10.1
8	3.2	5.0
9	1.2	1.5
10	1.3	2.4

Even though the problem requires a graphical solution, we can illustrate the use of the **Beta Estimation** submodule using the above data. The determination of the solution without the help from the software package is out of the scope of this text.

The following data need to be entered to obtain the beta of Hartford (note that there are two different input screens):

Screen 1

Number of Observations   = 10

---

*Problem from *Fundamentals of Investments* by Gordon J. Alexander and William F. Sharpe. © 1989 by Prentice Hall, Inc. Reprinted with permission from Prentice Hall, Inc.

After the above data are entered, highlight **Input Percent Returns** and press the ⟨**Enter**⟩ key to bring up the next input screen. Enter the following data in the second input screen.

Observation # 1	8.1	8.0
Observation # 2	3.0	0.0
Observation # 3	5.3	14.9
Observation # 4	1.0	5.0
Observation # 5	−3.1	−4.1
Observation # 6	−3.0	−8.9
Observation # 7	5.0	10.1
Observation # 8	3.2	5.0
Observation # 9	1.2	1.5
Observation # 10	1.3	2.4

The data entry screen is shown in Figure 6.11. After ensuring that all data are entered correctly, highlight the choice **Show Results** in the menu bar and press the ⟨**Enter**⟩ key. This will bring up the solution shown in Figure 6.12, which presents the descriptive statistics of the Hartford Inc. stock and the market portfolio. The regression estimates can be brought up on the screen by highlighting **More Results** and pressing the ⟨**Enter**⟩ key. This screen is shown in Figure 6.13.

Fig. 6.11

```
┌─────────────────────────────────────────────────────────┐
│             Returns Data for Beta Estimation            │
│        Stock Returns               Market Returns       │
│    Obs. #   1:     8.10      Obs. #   1:     8.00       │
│    Obs. #   2:     3.00      Obs. #   2:     0.00       │
│    Obs. #   3:     5.30      Obs. #   3:    14.90       │
│    Obs. #   4:     1.00      Obs. #   4:     5.00       │
│    Obs. #   5:    -3.10      Obs. #   5:    -4.10       │
│    Obs. #   6:    -3.00      Obs. #   6:    -8.90       │
│    Obs. #   7:     5.00      Obs. #   7:    10.10       │
│    Obs. #   8:     3.20      Obs. #   8:     5.00       │
│    Obs. #   9:     1.20      Obs. #   9:     1.50       │
│    Obs. #  10     1.30       Obs. #  10:     2.40       │
└─────────────────────────────────────────────────────────┘
```

Please hit the <ENTER> key after entering data in each field

| Edit Input | Show Results

PORTFOLIO ANALYSIS

The rationale behind investing in a diversified portfolio instead of a single security is that a diversified portfolio is considerably less risky compared with a single security. This can be demonstrated by calculating the risk and the

Fig. 6.12

```
┌─────────────────────────────────────────────────────────┐
│         Descriptive Statistics of Returns Data (%)        │
│                                                           │
│  Arithmetic Mean Stock Return over the Period:    2.200   │
│                                                           │
│  Geometric Mean Stock Return over the Period:     2.145   │
│                                                           │
│  Standard Deviation of Stock Returns:             3.532   │
│                                                           │
│  Arithmetic Mean Market Return over the Period:   3.390   │
│                                                           │
│  Geometric Mean Market Return over the Period:    3.181   │
│                                                           │
│  Standard Deviation of Market Returns:            6.889   │
└─────────────────────────────────────────────────────────┘
```

```
┌──────────────────┐
│  Print Results   │                    Next Results Screen
└──────────────────┘
```

expected return of a portfolio of made up of two risky securities, using the following general models, with $n = 2$:

$$R_p = \sum_{i=1}^{n} w_i R_i$$

$$\sigma_p = \sqrt{\sum_{i=1}^{n} \sum_{j=1}^{n} w_i\, w_j\, \sigma_{ij}}$$

The calculation of the standard deviation of returns from a portfolio from the above model can quickly get very complicated. As the number of securities in the portfolio increases, the number of terms which have to be summed up to obtain the portfolio standard deviation increase in a geometrical proportion. The **Portfolio Analysis** submodule reduces this task to that of simple data entry.

The expected return and the standard deviation calculation requires the input of the following variables:

Fig. 6.13

```
┌─────────────────────────────────────────────────────────┐
│                   Regression Results                      │
│                                                           │
│        The Intercept Term (Alpha):       0.007            │
│                                                           │
│        The Standard Error of Alpha:      0.007            │
│                                                           │
│        Beta of the Stock:                0.433            │
│                                                           │
│        The Standard Error of Beta:       0.097            │
│                                                           │
│        R Squared Statistic:              0.714            │
└─────────────────────────────────────────────────────────┘
```

```
┌──────────────────┐
│  Print Results   │  Previous Screen  Edit Input  New Input Port. Menu
└──────────────────┘
```

1. the expected return from each security in the portfolio;
2. the standard deviation of each security in the portfolio;
3. the fraction of the portfolio invested in each security; and
4. either the covariance or the correlation coefficient between returns from each pair of the securities in the portfolio.

The user may enter the data either in the form of a covariance matrix or a correlation coefficient matrix.

To access this submodule from the **Portfolio Theory** menu, highlight the selection **Portfolio Analysis** and press the ⟨**Enter**⟩ key. This will bring up the first data entry screen in the submodule.

Sample Problem

Given the variance-covariance matrix for three securities, as well as the percentage of the portfolio that each security comprises, calculate the portfolio's standard deviation.*

	Security A	*Security B*	*Security C*
Security A	459	− 211	112
Security B	− 211	312	215
Security C	112	215	179
	$X_a = 0.30$	$X_b = 0.50$	$X_c = 0.20$

The variance of the portfolio returns can be found from the following calculation:

$$\sigma^2 = .3 \times .3 \times 459 + .5 \times .3 \times (-211) + .3 \times .2 \times 112$$
$$+ \ldots + \ldots + \ldots + .2 \times .2 \times 179$$
$$= 119.62$$

The standard deviation of the portfolio returns is simply the square-root of the above result, equal to 10.94 percent.

To obtain the software solution of the problem, the data need to be entered in three stages. The first data input screen will information about the data input format (covariance matrix or correlation matrix) and the number of securities in the portfolio.

Screen 1

Number of Stocks in the Portfolio   = 3

After the above data are entered (as shown in Figure 6.14), highlight **Covariance Matrix** (since the data are provided as a covariance matrix) and press the ⟨**Enter**⟩ key to bring up the next input screen. Enter the following data in the second input screen. You will notice that this screen requires data about

*Problem from *Fundamentals of Investments* by Gordon J. Alexander and William F. Sharpe. © 1989 by Prentice Hall, Inc. Reprinted with permission from Prentice Hall, Inc.

stock returns, which are not furnished in the problem. You may enter any number for returns, including zeros.

Screen 2

	Rate of Return	Weight in Portfolio
Stock 1	0	30
Stock 2	0	50
Stock 3	0	20

The second input screen after data entry is shown in Figure 6.15. Follow the same procedure as above to bring up the third data input screen. This screen will require you to input the covariances of the securities. Since the covariance matrix is always symmetric, the data input matrix is designed such that you need to input only the unique data. Those data which need not be input are marked with an XXX in the place of entry.

Screen 3

	Asset 1	Asset 2	Asset 3
Asset 1	459	XXX	XXX
Asset 2	−211	312	XXX
Asset 3	112	215	179

The third data entry screen is shown in Figure 6.16. After ensuring that all data are entered correctly, highlight the choice **Show Results** in the menu bar and press the ⟨**Enter**⟩ key. This will bring up the solution shown in Figure 6.17.

Sample Problem

Listed here are estimates of the standard deviations and correlation coefficients for three stocks.*

Stock	Standard Deviation	Correlation with Stock		
		A	B	C
A	12%	1.00	−1.00	0.20
B	15	−1.00	1.00	0.60
C	10	0.20	0.60	1.00

a. .....

b. If the portfolio is comprised of 30 percent of stock A, 30 percent of stock B, and 40 percent of stock C, what is the portfolio standard deviation?

As before, the solution procedure is to calculate the portfolio variance:

$$\sigma^2 = 0.30 \times 0.30 \times 12 \times 12 + 0.30 \times 0.40 \times 12 \times 15 \times (-1.00)$$
$$+ \ldots + \ldots + \ldots + 0.40 \times 0.40 \times 10 \times 10$$
$$= 44.17$$

*Problem from *Fundamentals of Investments* by Gordon J. Alexander and William F. Sharpe. © 1989 by Prentice Hall, Inc. Reprinted with permission from Prentice Hall, Inc.

Fig. 6.14

```
+-------------------------------------------------+
|                                                 |
|              Portfolio Analysis                 |
|                                                 |
|         Number of Data Points:    3             |
|                                                 |
+-------------------------------------------------+
```

Please hit the <ENTER> key after entering data in each field

```
+--------------+
| Edit Input   |          Covariance Matrix      Corr. Coeff. Matrix
+--------------+
```

Fig. 6.15

```
+-----------------------------------------------------------+
|                 Portfolio Analysis Data                   |
|                                                           |
|            Rate of Return  Weight in                      |
|                 (%)        Portfolio (%)                  |
|   Asset 1       0.00          30.00                       |
|                                                           |
|   Asset 2       0.00          50.00                       |
|                                                           |
|   Asset 3       0.00          20.00                       |
|                                                           |
+-----------------------------------------------------------+
```

Please hit the <ENTER> key after entering data in each field

```
+--------------+
| Edit Input   |          Expected Return   Next Input Screen
+--------------+
```

Fig. 6.16

```
+-----------------------------------------------------------+
|                  Covariance Matrix                        |
|                  Asset 1      Asset 2      Asset 3         |
|                                                           |
|    Asset 1       459.00       XXXXX        XXXXX           |
|                                                           |
|    Asset 2      -211.00       312.00       XXXXX           |
|                                                           |
|    Asset 3       112.00       215.00       179.00          |
|                                                           |
+-----------------------------------------------------------+
```

```
+--------------+
| Edit Input   |                                 Show Results
+--------------+
```

Fig. 6.17

```
+-----------------------------------------------------------+
|              Portfolio Analysis Results                   |
|                                                           |
|   Expected Return from the Portfolio (%):      0.00       |
|                                                           |
|   Standard Deviation of the Portfolio (%):    10.94       |
|                                                           |
+-----------------------------------------------------------+
```

```
+---------------+
| Print Results |    Edit Input   New Input   Portfolio Menu
+---------------+
```

The portfolio standard deviation is the square-root of the above result and is equal to 6.65 percent.

The data input process to obtain the software solution of this problem is similar to that described above with one exception. This problem provides data about the correlation coefficient matrix instead of the covariance matrix. The first data input screen will accept information about the data input format (covariance matrix or correlation matrix) and the number of securities in the portfolio.

Screen 1

Number of Stocks in the Portfolio   = 3

This problem provides stock data as a correlation coefficient matrix. Therefore, highlight **Corr. Coeff. Matrix** and press the ⟨**Enter**⟩ key to bring up the suitable data entry screen.

Enter the following data in the second input screen. You will notice that this screen requires data about stock returns, which are not furnished in the problem. You may enter any number for returns, including zeros, because the magnitude of returns have no effect on the desired solution.

Screen 2

	Rate of Return	*Wgt. in Port.*	*Std. Dev.*
Stock 1	0	30	12
Stock 2	0	30	15
Stock 3	0	40	10

The second input screen after data entry is shown in Figure 6.18. Follow the same procedure as above to bring up the third data input screen. This screen will require you to input the correlation coefficients of the securities. Since this matrix is also always symmetric, the data input matrix is designed such that you need to input only the unique data. This also minimizes the number of data items to be entered. Those data which need not be input are marked with an XXXX in the place of entry.

Fig. 6.18

```
┌─────────────────────────────────────────────────────────────┐
│                   Portfolio Analysis Data                     │
│                                                               │
│           Rate of Return   Weight in      Standard Deviation  │
│               (%)          Portfolio (%)      (%)             │
│   Asset 1     0.00            30.00          12.00            │
│                                                               │
│   Asset 2     0.00            40.00          15.00            │
│                                                               │
│   Asset 3     0.00            30.00          10.00            │
│                                                               │
└─────────────────────────────────────────────────────────────┘
```

```
    Please hit the <ENTER> key after entering data in each field
   ┌──────────────┐
   │  Edit Input  │        Expected Return   Next Input Screen
   └──────────────┘
```

Fig. 6.19

```
┌─────────────────────────────────────────────────────┐
│      Correlation Coefficient Matrix (Decimals)       │
│               Asset 1⌐   Asset 2    Asset 3           │
│                                                       │
│    Asset 1       1.00      XXXXX      XXXXX           │
│                                                       │
│    Asset 2      -1.00      1.00       XXXXX           │
│                                                       │
│    Asset 3       0.20      0.60       1.00            │
│                                                       │
└─────────────────────────────────────────────────────┘
```

```
┌──────────────────┐
│   Edit Input      │                          Show Results
└──────────────────┘
```

Screen 3

	Asset 1	*Asset 2*	*Asset 3*
Asset 1	1.00	XXXX	XXXX
Asset 2	−1.00	1.00	XXXX
Asset 3	0.20	0.60	1.00

The third data entry screen is shown in Figure 6.19. After ensuring that all data are entered correctly, highlight the choice **Show Results** in the menu bar and press the ⟨**Enter**⟩ key. This will bring up the solution shown in Figure 6.20.

SECURITY MARKET LINE

The Security Market Line (SML), also known as the Capital Asset Pricing Model, is the representation of the relationship between the equilibrium expected rate of return from a security and its systematic risk. The systematic risk of the security is measured by its beta coefficient. The model is:

$$R_i = R_f + B_i (R_m - R_f)$$

The equilibrium expected rate of return from a security consists of two components: the risk-free rate of return and the security risk premium. The security risk premium, in turn, varies in direct proportion with the beta coefficient of the security and the market risk premium, $R_m - R_f$.

Fig. 6.20

```
┌─────────────────────────────────────────────────────┐
│              Portfolio Analysis Results               │
│                                                       │
│   Expected Return from the Portfolio (%):    0.00     │
│                                                       │
│   Standard Deviation of the Portfolio (%):   6.65     │
│                                                       │
└─────────────────────────────────────────────────────┘
```

```
┌──────────────────┐
│  Print Results    │     Edit Input    New Input    Portfolio Menu
└──────────────────┘
```

This submodule can be accessed from the **Portfolio Theory** menu by selecting **Security Market Line** and pressing the ⟨**Enter**⟩ key.

Sample Problem

You expect the RFR to be 0.10 and the market return to be 0.14. Compute the expected return for the following stocks:*

Stock	Beta
U	0.85
N	1.25
D	−0.20

The calculations involved in solving this problem are relatively simple.

$$R_U = 0.10 + 0.85 \times (0.14 - 0.10) = 0.134$$
$$R_N = 0.10 + 1.20 \times (0.14 - 0.10) = 0.148$$
$$R_D = 0.10 - 0.20 \times (0.14 - 0.10) = 0.092$$

To obtain the solution to this problem using the software, enter the following data (first, for stock U):

Risk-free Rate	= 10
Return on Market Portfolio	= 14
Beta of the Security	= 0.85

The data input screen is shown in Figure 6.21. Highlight the choice **Show Results** and press the ⟨**Enter**⟩ key to bring up the solution screen, which will appear as shown in Figure 6.22.

Since two of the three input variables are the same for all three stocks, the solution to the next part of the problem, rate of return on stock N, is easier to obtain by changing the beta of the security in the data entry screen. To enter the edit mode from the solution screen, highlight the choice **Edit Input** in the

Fig. 6.21

```
            Required Rate of Return from SML

        Risk-free Rate of Return (%):   10.00

      Return on Market Portfolio (%):   14.00

               Beta of the Security:    0.85
```

Please hit the <ENTER> key after entering data in each field

```
Edit Input
```
                                              Show Results

---

*Problem from *Investments* by Frank K. Reilly. © 1986 by CBS College Publishing. Reprinted with permission from The Dryden Press.

Fig. 6.22

```
┌─────────────────────────────────────────────────────────┐
│ ┌─────────────────────────────────────────────────────┐ │
│ │          Required Rate of Return -SML               │ │
│ │                                                     │ │
│ │  1. Market Risk Premium (%) = Rm - Rf =      4.00   │ │
│ │                                                     │ │
│ │  2. Risk Premium on the Security = B(Rm-Rf) =  3.40 │ │
│ │                                                     │ │
│ │  3. Required Rate of Return (%) = Rf+B(Rm-Rf) = 13.40│ │
│ └─────────────────────────────────────────────────────┘ │
└─────────────────────────────────────────────────────────┘
```

Please hit the <ENTER> key after entering data in each field

```
┌──────────────────┐
│  Print Results   │     Edit Input    New Input    Portfolio Menu
└──────────────────┘
```

menu bar at the bottom of the screen and press the ⟨**Enter**⟩ key. This will bring up the data entry screen with the data for stock U in place. Use the down arrow key to position the cursor on the third field, beta of the security, and change it to "1.20," the beta of stock N. Press the ⟨**Enter**⟩ key to bring up the menu bar once again. Highlight the choice **Show Results** and press the ⟨**Enter**⟩ key to bring up the solution for stock N. Repeat this process to enter the beta for stock D and obtain the solution for stock D.

To move on to the next sample problem, highlight the choice **New Input** in the menu bar and press the ⟨**Enter**⟩ key. This will bring up the data entry screen.

Sample Problem

Assume that the SML is given as $R_i = 0.04 + 0.08B$ and the estimated betas of two stocks are $B_x = 0.5$ and $B_y = 2.0$. What must the expected return on the two securities be in order for one feel that they are a good purchase?*

The equilibrium rate of return provided by the SML is the minimum rate of return an investor should accept from a security. So, in order that one feels that the two stocks are good purchases, the minimum rate of return on each of the two stocks should be the one calculated using the SML.

$$R_x = 0.04 + 0.08 \times 0.5 = 0.08$$
$$R_y = 0.04 + 0.08 \times 2.0 = 0.20$$

To solve the problem using the software, enter the following data:

Risk-free Rate	= 4 (from the SML equation)
Return on Market Portfolio	= 12 (8 + 4 = 12 from the SML equation)
Beta of the Security	= 0.50

The data entry screen is shown in Figure 6.23. Highlight the choice **Show Results** and press the ⟨**Enter**⟩ key. This will bring up the solution shown in Figure 6.24.

*Problem from *Security Analysis and Portfolio Management* by Donald E. Fischer and Ronald J. Jordan. © 1991 by Prentice Hall, Inc. Reprinted with permission from Prentice Hall, Inc.

Fig. 6.23

```
┌─────────────────────────────────────────────────┐
│  ┌───────────────────────────────────────────┐  │
│  │     Required Rate of Return from SML       │  │
│  │                                            │  │
│  │   Risk-free Rate of Return (%):    4.00    │  │
│  │                                            │  │
│  │  Return on Market Portfolio (%):  12.00    │  │
│  │                                            │  │
│  │         Beta of the Security:    0.50      │  │
│  └───────────────────────────────────────────┘  │
└─────────────────────────────────────────────────┘
```

Please hit the <ENTER> key after entering data in each field

```
┌──────────────┐
│  Edit Input  │                          Show Results
└──────────────┘
```

The second part of the problem, R_y, can be solved using a procedure similar to the one described in sample problem 1 in this section.

To return to the data entry screen, highlight the choice **New Input** and press the ⟨**Enter**⟩ key.

Sample Problem

Given that the expected return on the market portfolio is 12 percent, the risk-free rate of return is 6 percent, the beta of stock A is .85 and the beta of stock B is 1.20.*

What are the equilibrium returns from stocks A and B?

The equilibrium expected return for stock A = 6 + 0.85 × (12 − 6)
= 11.1 percent
The equilibrium expected return for stock B = 6 + 1.2 × (12 − 6)
= 13.2 percent

Fig. 6.24

```
┌─────────────────────────────────────────────────────────┐
│         Required Rate of Return -SML                     │
│                                                          │
│   1. Market Risk Premium (%) = Rm - Rf =         8.00    │
│                                                          │
│   2. Risk Premium on the Security = B(Rm-Rf) =   4.00    │
│                                                          │
│   3. Required Rate of Return (%) = Rf+B(Rm-Rf) = 8.00    │
└─────────────────────────────────────────────────────────┘
```

Please hit the <ENTER> key after entering data in each field

```
┌───────────────┐
│ Print Results │    Edit Input    New Input    Portfolio Menu
└───────────────┘
```

*Problem from *Fundamentals of Investments* by Gordon J. Alexander and William F. Sharpe. © 1989 by Prentice Hall, Inc. Reprinted with permission from Prentice Hall, Inc.

Fig. 6.25

```
┌─────────────────────────────────────────────────────────┐
│ ┌─────────────────────────────────────────────────────┐ │
│ │         Required Rate of Return from SML             │ │
│ │                                                     │ │
│ │      Risk-free Rate of Return (%):    6.00          │ │
│ │                                                     │ │
│ │   Return on Market Portfolio (%):   12.00           │ │
│ │                                                     │ │
│ │             Beta of the Security:    0.85           │ │
│ └─────────────────────────────────────────────────────┘ │
└─────────────────────────────────────────────────────────┘
```

```
        Please hit the <ENTER> key after entering data in each field
      ┌──────────────┐
      │  Edit Input  │                          Show Results
      └──────────────┘
```

To solve this problem using the software, enter the data for stock A first:

Risk-free Rate of Return   = 6

Return on Market Portfolio   = 12

Beta of the Security   = 0.85

The screen will appear as in Figure 6.25. Highlight the choice **Show Results** and press the ⟨**Enter**⟩ key. The solution screen will appear as shown in Figure 6.26.

To solve for the equilibrium expected rate of return from stock B, enter the edit mode from the solution screen using the procedure described in sample problem 1 of this section and edit the beta field to "1.20." Highlight **Show Results** once again and press the ⟨**Enter**⟩ key to bring up the solution for stock B.

MINIMUM RISK PORTFOLIO

Two individually risky securities can be combined to form a portfolio which may be less risky than either of the two securities. It is possible to minimize the portfolio risk (standard deviation of returns) by carefully selecting the fractions of the portfolio to be invested in the two securities. This sub-module

Fig. 6.26

```
┌─────────────────────────────────────────────────────────────┐
│ ┌─────────────────────────────────────────────────────────┐ │
│ │            Required Rate of Return −SML                 │ │
│ │                                                         │ │
│ │  1. Market Risk Premium (%) = Rm − Rf =          6.00   │ │
│ │                                                         │ │
│ │  2. Risk Premium on the Security = B(Rm−Rf) =    5.10   │ │
│ │                                                         │ │
│ │  3. Required Rate of Return (%) = Rf+B(Rm−Rf) = 11.10   │ │
│ └─────────────────────────────────────────────────────────┘ │
└─────────────────────────────────────────────────────────────┘
```

```
        Please hit the <ENTER> key after entering data in each field
      ┌────────────────┐
      │ Print Results  │   Edit Input    New Input    Portfolio Menu
      └────────────────┘
```

allows an investor to determine the fractions of investment in the two securities which will minimize the portfolio risk. It will also calculate the portfolio risk.

The formula for the risk minimizing investment in security 1 is

$$W_1 = \frac{\sigma_2^2 - \sigma_{12}}{\sigma_1^2 + \sigma_2^2 - 2\sigma_{12}}$$

The investment fraction in security 2 is

$$W_2 = 1 - W_1$$

This submodule can be accessed from the **Portfolio Theory** menu by selecting **Minimum Risk Portfolio** and pressing the ⟨**Enter**⟩ key. The data entry screen for the submodule will appear.

Sample Problem

Security 1 has a standard deviation of returns of 12 percent. Security 2 has a standard deviation of returns of 14 percent. The correlation coefficient between their returns is -1.00. Calculate the weights of these securities in the minimum risk portfolio. Also calculate the standard deviation of returns for the minimum risk portfolio.

The analytical solution to this problem is

$W_1 = (14 \times 14 - (-1.00) \times 12 \times 14) \div (12 \times 12 + 14 \times 14 - 12 \times 12 \times 14 \times (-1))$
$\quad = 0.5385$, and
$W_2 = 0.4615.$

The standard deviation of this portfolio is

$\sigma* = 0.5385 \times 0.5384 \times 12 \times 12 + 0.4615 \times 0.4615 \times 14 \times 14 + 2 \times 0.5385 \times 0.4615 \times 12 \times 14 \times (-1.00)$
$\quad = 0.00$

To obtain the software solution of this problem, the following data are needed:

1. Standard Deviation of Returns from Security 1 = 12
2. Standard Deviation of Returns from Security 2 = 14
3. Correlation Coefficient between the Returns   = −1.00

Fig. 6.27

```
┌──────────────────────────────────────────────────────────────┐
│           Minimum Risk Portfolio of Two Securities           │
│                                                              │
│   Standard Deviation of Returns from Security 1 (%): 12.000  │
│                                                              │
│   Standard Deviation of Returns from Security 2 (%): 14.000  │
│                                                              │
│       Correlation Coefficient between the Returns: -1.000    │
└──────────────────────────────────────────────────────────────┘
```

Please hit the <ENTER> key after entering data in each field

```
┌─────────────────┐
│   Edit Input    │                              Show Results
└─────────────────┘
```

Fig. 6.28

```
┌─────────────────────────────────────────────────────────────┐
│                  Minimum Risk Portfolio                      │
│  1. Proportion of Portfolio in Security 1 =      0.5385      │
│                                                               │
│  2. Proportion of Portfolio in Security 2 =      0.4615      │
│                                                               │
│  3. Standard Deviation of Returns from Portfolio (%)= 0.000  │
└─────────────────────────────────────────────────────────────┘
```

┌─────────────────┐
│ Print Results   │   Edit Input   New Input   FM Menu
└─────────────────┘

Enter these data in the data input screen. The screen will appear as shown in Figure 6.27. Highlight **Show Results** in the menu bar and press the ⟨**Enter**⟩ key. This would bring up the solution screen shown in Figure 6.28.

To exit this submodule highlight **Portfolio Menu** in the menu bar at the bottom of the solution screen and press the ⟨**Enter**⟩ key. This will return the control of the program to the main menu in the portfolio analysis section. Highlight **Portfolio Performance** in this menu and press the ⟨**Enter**⟩ key to access that submodule.

PORTFOLIO PERFORMANCE EVALUATION

An investor has to be careful when comparing performances of different investments. The proper way to compare the performance of different investments is to estimate a performance measure based on the risk-adjusted returns from those investments. Two of the best known portfolio performance measures are Reward to Variability Ratio (Sharpe Index) and Reward to Volatility Ratio (Treynor Index). This submodule allows a student to compare the performances of two portfolios by estimating these ratios for each of the portfolios.

These ratios are defined as follows:

$$\text{Sharpe Index} = (r_i - r_f)/\sigma, \text{ and}$$
$$\text{Treynor Index} = (r_i - r_f)/B.$$

Sample Problem

The following table presents data over a five year period on two mutual funds, the Jupiter Fund and the Saturn Fund:

	Jupiter Fund	*Saturn Fund*
Average Monthly Return	1.67%	1.75%
Standard Deviation of Returns	2.27%	2.76%
Beta	1.04	1.12

The average monthly risk free rate during this period was 0.57 percent. Based on the above information, indicate which fund was the superior performer over the five-year period.*

The analytical solution will be to calculate the two performance measures discussed above:

	Jupiter Fund	*Saturn Fund*
Sharpe Index	(1.67 − .57)/2.27	(1.75 − .57)/2.76
	0.4846	0.4275
Treynor Index	(1.67 − .57)/1.04	(1.75 − .57)/1.12
	1.0577	1.0536

Both the performance measures indicate that the Jupiter Fund provides the investor a slightly higher rate of return because the risks of the portfolios are equalized. Therefore, it is the superior performer.

To obtain these results using the software, the following data are relevant:

	Portfolio #1	*Portfolio #2*
Rate of Return	1.67	1.75
Standard Deviation of Returns	2.27	2.76
Beta	1.04	1.12
Risk-free Rate	0.57	

The data input screen will appear as in Figure 6.29 after data entry. Highlight **Show Results** and press the ⟨**Enter**⟩ key to bring up the solution screen which is shown in Figur 6.30.

Fig. 6.29

```
┌──────────────────────────────────────────────────────────────┐
│              Portfolio Performance Evaluation                  │
│                                                                │
│                         Portfolio      Portfolio               │
│                            #1             #2                   │
│                                                                │
│        Rate of Return (%):    1.67           1.75             │
│                                                                │
│   Std. Dev. of Returns (%):   2.27           2.76             │
│                                                                │
│                     Beta:     1.04           1.12             │
│                                                                │
│           Risk Free Rate (%):        0.57                     │
│                                                                │
└──────────────────────────────────────────────────────────────┘
```

Please hit the <ENTER> key after entering data in each field

┌─────────────────┐
│   Edit Input   │   Show Results
└─────────────────┘

*Problem from *Fundamentals of Investments* by Gordon J. Alexander and William F. Sharpe. © 1989 by Prentice Hall, Inc. Reprinted with permission from Prentice Hall, Inc.

Fig. 6.30

```
╔══════════════════════════════════════════════════════════╗
║           Portfolio Performance Evaluation               ║
║                                                          ║
║                          Portfolio #1     Portfolio #2   ║
║  1. Risk Premium (%) = Ri-Rf =    1.10         1.18      ║
║                                                          ║
║  2. Sharpe Index = (Ri-Rf)/σ =    0.48         0.43      ║
║                                                          ║
║  3. Treynor Index = (Ri-Rf)/ß =   1.06         1.05      ║
╚══════════════════════════════════════════════════════════╝
```

┌─────────────────┐
│ Print Results │   Edit Input   New Input   FM Menu
└─────────────────┘

This concludes the discussion of the **Portfolio Theory** module. To exit this module highlight **Portfolio Menu** in the menu bar at the bottom of the solution screen and press the ⟨**Enter**⟩ key. This will return the control of the program to the main menu in the portfolio analysis section. Highlight the choice **Investment Problems Menu** and press the ⟨**Enter**⟩ key. The control will be passed on to the main menu.